BEFORE YOU SAY A WORD:
The Executive Guide to Effective
Communication

BEFORE YOU SAY A WORD:
The Executive Guide to Effective Communication

Myles Martel, Ph.D.

Prentice-Hall, Inc.
Englewood Cliffs, New Jersey

Prentice-Hall International, Inc., *London*
Prentice-Hall of Australia, Pty. Ltd., *Sydney*
Prentice-Hall Canada Inc., *Toronto*
Prentice-Hall of India Private Ltd., *New Delhi*
Prentice-Hall of Japan, Inc., *Toyko*
Prentice-Hall of Southeast Asia Pte. Ltd., *Singapore*
Whitehall Books, Ltd., Wellington, *New Zealand*
Editora Prentice-Hall do Brasil, Ltda., *Rio de Janeiro*

© 1984 by
Prentice-Hall, Inc.
Englewood Cliffs, N.J.

Library of Congress Cataloging in Publication Data

Martel, Myles.
  Before you say a word.

  Includes index.
1. Communication in management.   I. Title.
HD30.3.M37   1983   658.4'5   83-16130
ISBN 0-13-071613-8

Printed in the United States of America

Also by Myles Martel

Political Campaign Debates: Images, Strategies, and Tactics

Dedication

To my wife, Susan, whose encouragement is valued more than any communication consultant or wordsmith can capture, and to my mother, Sadye, who always seemed to understand my appetite for knowledge and expression.

Preface

Since forming my own consulting firm in 1969, I have become increasingly aware of how little published advice the executive has to rely on as he prepares for both public and internal engagements. Over the years superficial and absolutistic advice—tiresome bromides—have to a significant extent permeated the executive suite: "Always look into the T.V. camera," "Answer not the question asked by the reporter, but rather the one you want to answer," and "If you're nervous, focus on a friendly face throughout your speech."

Well-intentioned advice for sure. But hardly substantial. Struck by the realization that executives in their demanding daily pace are all too susceptible to following the advice of tipsters disguised as consultants, I decided to write this book, a comprehensive reflection of my consultative approach which can be summarized as follows:

> *To help the executive develop a system that focuses on both substance and image for any type of engagement—a system that helps insure his control, confidence, clarity, credibility and persuasiveness.*

Establishing the system is not difficult. A firm commitment by the executive is all that is required. And from the commitment will spring a sense of mastery over any type of engagement. This mastery will not only enhance the executive's communication skill, but will, as well, strengthen both his image and his impact as a leader.

Acknowledgments

So many friends have provided concepts and suggestions that have inspired my confidence in the importance of this book and strengthened its usefulness.

Before I say another word, I must acknowledge the invaluable assistance of Corey Sandler, a New York editor and writer.

I am also grateful to the following associates of my firm:

To Dick Mendenhall for his excellent suggestions regarding the chapter on TV Talk Shows.

To Gene Harris for his able insights regarding the chapter on Media Interviews.

To Phil Toman whose command of the Crisis Communication principles reflected in Chapter 18 ranks him as one of the best in his field.

To Joe Malatesta and Richard Spiegleman for providing much of the material that resulted in the section on testimony contained in Chapter 20.

Other friends who have provided ideas and examples include Tom Bender, Rose Bisciotti, Jeff Close, John Field, Rich Heaton, Carolyn Keefe, Norm Kennard, Lou Stone, Jera Stribling, Barry Pierce, Fred Stern, and Carl Voss.

To the following persons (listed alphabetically) who provided consulting environments for me to test and acquire so many of the concepts presented in this book:

Floyd Alston	Jerry Crop	Dick Evans
Earl Baker	Alex Cushman	Blaine Fabian
Michel Besson	Frank Daniels	Ed Forst, Jr.
Charlie Black	Mitch Daniels	Tom Gill
George Butler	Kathy Donahue	Jack Green
Les Butler	Elise DuPont	Carl Gustin

Kemp Harshman
Alan Hill
Alan Hoffman
Joe Jones
Wally Judd
Loren Kaye
Ben Key
Ron Lauder
Joe La Sala
Tony Loscalzo
George Metzger
Dan Molesky
Bob Muilenberg
Jeff Perkins
Andy Poat

Henry Pollak
Robert Pollak
Dennis Randall
Walter Reed
David Rights
Bob Rike
Charles Rockey
Tony Santilli
Dick Schulze
Norm Sherlock
Frank Simpson
Richard Simpson
Alex Smith
Floyd Smith
Jay Snider

Barbara Sokoloff
Tom Spruance
Bob Stevens
Lee Swartz
P. John Taylor
Carol Tokar
Bruce Trainor
Frank Ursomarso
Bill Verrochi
Dottie Wackerman
Pen Waggoner
Joe Walsh
George Westerman
Joe Westner
Dick Wirthlin

To Richard Lampert who, without my knowing it, but to my absolute delight, persuasively passed on to Prentice-Hall my interest in writing this book.

To my friends at Prentice-Hall, David Wright, Ruth Krieger and Brianne Carey, whose professionalism, warmth and insightfulness were a constant source of confidence and guidance. I feel truly privileged to have worked with such a fine team.

To my five-year-old son, David, who, through his magnificent curiosity and well-tuned communicative skills, has helped me to cultivate my own ability to listen, question, define, and disclose.

Finally, to my wife, Susan, who determinedly convinced me as I was completing another book—a five-year labor of love and every other conceivable emotion—that I should write this one.

INTRODUCTION

Wait! Before you say a word, answer this question: *Why?*

As a business person, you cannot afford to spend valuable time in mere personal indulgence.

- What is your purpose?
- Why do you want to speak, and what do you hope will result?
- What do you want your audience to do?

One of the modern tests of an executive must be his or her ability to inspire, persuade, inform and answer to the public, the media, the stockholders, the regulatory agencies and the workforce.

To put it another way: management *is* communication. It is developing and disseminating a message with a defined goal in mind.

Your company needs to secure products; it needs to attract buyers. It must make the local, state and federal governments aware of its problems; it must keep government from interfering unduly in its business. And, of course, your company needs to talk with, and listen to, your employees.

Communication is also a function of democracy, an essential element of the marketplace of ideas. Your business is a part of that economy, too, in its dealings as a corporate citizen in society.

Why is it important, then, that your company—and you as an executive—communicate effectively? Think of it in terms of cost-effectiveness.

The basic premise of this book is that an executive needs a system for every type of engagement, using carefully thought-out communication skills. There are no tricks or gimmicks. The key to success in communication is hard work; there is no such thing as too much attention to detail.

It's not just lonely at the top; it's insecure. The pinnacle is a very narrow place, with nowhere to go to avoid the demands of communication. And, for many executives, being the principal spokesperson is different from anything else done in his or her career.

Today's executive must be able to express himself or herself clearly, to demonstrate personal and corporate credibility, remain accessible, show responsiveness—and still find time to manage the company.

ORAL VS. WRITTEN COMMUNICATION

There are many, many ways to communicate a message—it seems as though a new variation on the old themes is developed every day. This book will deal primarily with oral or spoken communication in many different situations: the speech; the presentation; the sales briefing; meetings; testimony; question-and-answer sessions; media relations including newspaper, television and radio interviews; television and radio talk shows, panels and debates.

Writing a book, memo, or letter is very different from speaking your message. Each has its inherent strengths and risks.

Any mistake put into print is there forever, or at least for as long as the paper is kept. Like oral presentation, a written message must fight for the audience's attention. However, when you transmit that piece of paper to a reader, it is very difficult if not impossible to determine immediately how well the message is understood, or even whether there is any communication at all.

If you speak your message, you have the opportunity to fight for the listener's attention, to work to hold it, to determine if a message is coming across, and to modify your content and delivery to make it more effective.

And so, you are left with two other avenues of communication:

1. The speech or group presentation, or
2. The use of the mass media as intermediary.

The mass media, though, do blur some of the distinctions between the oral and written modes; in many instances you are forced to rely upon your ability to communicate in an oral fashion to someone who will then turn around and restate, in written or electronic form, what he or she believes your message to be.

For many executives—and persons in all walks of life—the need to present a prepared oral message brings on great crushing waves of fear, regardless of whether the executive has already demonstrated ability, credibility, self-confidence and sense of command.

But here's the secret: delivering a speech or making a presentation or handling a reporter or a talk show host are abilities almost anyone can learn. Indeed, these are largely learnable skills.

Later in the book, I'll discuss in detail speech anxiety and numerous practical principles to help you in specific communication situations. You'll learn about the importance of breaking the ice, how to take the fullest advantage of your own skills and background, and how to tap the resources of your staff, libraries, electronic data bases and professional organizations. And, in the final analysis, you will learn how to *master and enjoy the mastery* you will develop in addressing all types of situations—from the most basic to the most challenging.

Myles Martel
Bryn Mawr, Pennsylvania

TABLE OF CONTENTS

PART 1

Basic Principles

CHAPTER 1

Learning to Listen

Learning to listen—that's an unusual way to begin a book about learning to speak, isn't it?

It's not a frivolous matter, though. We must always bear in mind that communication is not a one-way process. Just as we can speak but not communicate, we can hear but not listen. What is meant by "listening"? Listening involves three major processes: first, receiving your words; second, interpreting them, based on the experience, education and biases of the listener; third, evaluating your message, including your credibility.

Studies have shown that listening is the primary communication activity in our lives. Research cited by the Sperry Corporation (in an important series of public service advertisements and brochures presented by the company) claims we spend about 80 percent of our waking hours involved in communication. Of that time 45 percent is devoted to listening, 30 percent to speaking, 16 percent to reading, and 9 percent to writing.

But we're also rather inefficient at our most common task. In one study, subjects were asked to listen to a ten-minute oral presentation and were tested immediately afterwards. The average listener heard, understood, evaluated properly and retained only about half of what was said. In tests made again after 48 hours, the amount retained dropped again by half. To put it another way, after two days the average listener could comprehend and remember only about one-fourth of what was said to him in a ten-minute presentation.

Sperry also reports that ideas get distorted by as much as 80 percent as they travel though a chain of command. Remember the "whispering down the lane" game we played as kids?

As a listener, you will project much of your feedback to the speaker by your body language. Think about some of the things you might do during a conversation that communicate *disinterest, impatience* or *prejudice:*

1. Not maintaining eye contact with the speaker, and looking at others or at objects.
2. Playing with keys, pens or other objects during a conversation.
3. Blocking your face with a notebook or newspaper or magazine during a conversation.
4. Walking away or turning from a person before the conversation has ended.
5. Accepting—or placing—phone calls during a conversation.
6. Exhibiting excessive or unnecessary nodding or grunting or body movements aimed at expediting completion of a conversation.
7. Discussing sensitive topics in the presence of uninvolved parties.
8. Remaining seated when approached by someone standing; remaining standing instead of encouraging a seated position when beginning a sensitive discussion that will require more than a few minutes.
9. Cutting a person off in mid-stream.

This is not meant to be a discussion of etiquette; nor is it intended to be a guide to listening to the next speech or conversation in which you participate. The point is that you should not attempt to enhance your skills as a speaker until you have given some thought to the process of *listening.* Listening well helps project your interest in others, politeness, sense of self-control, and other important qualities related to your leadership image within and outside your organization. But, more important, listening well gives you the information you need to lead.

So, then, how do you improve your listening? One way is to remedy the typical bad habits most of us have developed:*

> *The perceptual filter.* This is the sum total of preconceptions, prejudices, attitudes, motivation, personality and societal

---

*Many of these listening pitfalls were identified in studies by R.G. Nichols and L.A. Stevens in *Are You Listening?* McGraw-Hill, New York, 1957.

mores that can stand between the message you are hoping to send and the message that is received. Do you really think someone dressed in blue jeans and a t-shirt could receive an unfiltered hearing at a formal business meeting? How about a foreign student—an Iranian during the hostage crisis of 1980—who came to talk about foreign affairs? A senior colleague who wears cowboy boots to the board meeting?

Faking attention. Most people are aware that it is both rude and potentially damaging to your career to be perceived as "tuning out" on a conversation. The solution for many people, though, is to develop ways to appear attentive. Figuratively and sometimes literally, they sleep with their eyes open. Of course, the less proficient at this art give themselves away with their glassy, unresponsive stare.

Giving way to distractions. Good listeners are able to tune out "noise" and other interruptions to concentrate on content. An example might be a reporter who *must* listen to get the story, no matter what the circumstances. The ability to listen when equipment is running, phones are ringing, and voices are shouting back and forth requires commitment to concentration.

Listening only for the facts. As deadpan Sgt. Joe Friday used to say on "Dragnet," "Just the facts, ma'am." Tuning out ideas and conclusions can be a way to protect yourself from overload. You teach yourself to learn just enough to answer the question on a test or the specific demands of a specific job. But you'll be equally confused when all you can see are the trees and not the forest. "Big picture listening" is, therefore, the remedy.

Thinking about your response. Also known as "verbal battle," this is a habit born of argumentative situations. We've all been in a situation where we've been concentrating so much on what we will state or ask when we have the chance that we don't hear what the speaker is saying.

Writing everything down. The words go direct from your ears to your hand, virtually bypassing your brain. The listener tunes out all but "key words," and ends up missing the ideas.

False security. We normally speak at a rate of 125 to 150 words a minute. However, the brain can usually comprehend perhaps 400 words of non-technical spoken English per minute. As a result, we often find our brains racing ahead of the speaker. This is not necessarily a bad tendency, but it can lead to misunderstanding.

How do you improve your ability as a listener? First of all, by recognizing the importance of listening and deciding to work on the skill. Develop good habits; discard the bad ones. Rely on your mind's ability to process great amounts of information and exercise your mind.

Because we are able to think faster than we can speak, good listeners should use the time to try to anticipate what the speaker is going to say, to draw their own summaries and to formulate questions. The mere effort at "listening between the lines" should be of great help in becoming a better listener.

DEVELOPING A PERSONAL LISTENING EFFECTIVENESS PROGRAM

Here is a program you might undertake to improve your listening ability:

1. Be mentally and physically prepared to listen.
2. Think about the topic in advance if possible.
3. Concentrate all your physical and mental energy on listening.
4. Avoid interrupting the speaker when possible.
5. Demonstrate to the speaker your interest and alertness.
6. Look for areas of agreement.
7. Search for meanings and avoid arguing over choice of words.
8. Provide clear and unambiguous feedback.
9. Ask questions when you do not understand something.
10. Withhold evaluation of the message until the speaker is finished and you are sure you understand both the overall intent and the key elements of the message.

CHAPTER **2**

Non-Verbal
Communication—I See
What You're Saying

"I *see* what you're saying," someone may tell us after a conversation. Truer words may never have been spoken.

How much attention do you pay to the way you stand or sit or use your hands or configure your face? If you're like most people, you devote considerably more energy to *what* you say than to *how*. But consider this:

> In ordinary conversation between two persons words convey less than 35 percent of meaning. The remaining 65 percent of meaning is transmitted through non-verbal communication.*

No matter how carefully we research, prepare, choose our words and select our audience, two-thirds of what we communicate is derived from things we do rather than things we say. How do we hold our body? What gestures do we make? How are we dressed? What do we do to modify the tone of our voices? Where are our eyes focused during conversation?

---

*Ray L. Birdwhistell, cited by Mark L. Knapp, *Essentials of Nonverbal Communication*, Holt, Rinehart and Winston, New York, 1980, page 15.

TYPES OF NON-VERBAL BEHAVIOR

The various categories of non-verbal communication range from recognized "emblems" like the outstretched fingers of "V for Victory" to body odors to arrangement of furniture:*

Body motion or kinesic behavior: These include gestures, movements of the body, facial expressions, eye behavior (blinking, direction of gaze, and size and liveliness of pupils), and posture.

Emblems: These are nonverbal acts with a culturally recognized meaning; in our society these can range from circling of the ear with an outstretched finger ("He's nuts," the message reads), to fingers pinching off the nose ("It stinks"), to the more coarse, derogatory communication of an outstretched middle finger.

Illustrators: This connotes a picture of a word or image drawn with the hands or otherwise demonstrated by the speaker.

Regulators: These are signals that communicate when it is time for a speaker to continue, stop, hurry up, or explain his words. Slow, regular nodding of the head indicates agreement with what is being said. Quicker nodding means "Hurry up and finish."

Physical characteristics: These are characteristics that do not change during the course of a conversation—body shape, size, attractiveness, odors and the like.

Touching behavior: What is the effect on a conversation if one of the participants takes hold of the other's arm? His head? His neck?

Paralanguage: These are cues which deal with *how* words are spoken, including *vocal qualities, voice characterizers* (such as laughing, crying, yawning, clearing of the throat) and *voice segregates* such as the verbal pauses of "uh-huh" and similar indicators. As an example of the paralinguistic effects of voice quality, consider the phrase, "That's really smart." The voice can show appreciation or derision.

---

*Many of these categories were identified by Mark L. Knapp of Purdue University in his book, *Essentials of Nonverbal Communication*, Holt, Rinehart and Winston, New York, 1980.

Proxemics: The use and abuse of personal space. How close do you stand or sit in a conversation? How does speaking from behind a lectern differ from speaking without one? When do you leave your desk to meet with colleagues in the more intimate surroundings of your sofa, upholstered chairs, and coffee table—your informal conference area? What messages does this transmit regarding your respect for those attending? Strongly positives ones, for sure.

Chronemics: Communication through use of time. What is the meaning of silence or pauses in conversation? What is communicated by a speaker who arrives half an hour late for an engagement? By a speaker who delivers a five-minute presentation? A two-hour monologue? Chronemics communicates how organized you are as well as how busy and considerate you are. If you keep a person waiting 30 minutes for a scheduled appointment, what messages are you sending about yourself and possibly allowing him to infer about himself?

IT'S ALL IN THE EYES

It has long been said that "the eyes are the windows to the soul." They are also essential to you in establishing and maintaining credibility. ("Look me in the eye and say that," we say when we are attempting to determine a speaker's honesty.) An audience is more likely to believe a speaker who makes eye contact with it—and is more likely to believe that the words uttered are the speaker's own, and of deep conviction.

Eye contact is also critical to you as a speaker in determining the nature of the nonverbal messages being sent your way by the audience. The need for eye contact yields, therefore, a strong argument in favor of extemporaneous speaking for situations where you are not otherwise obliged to rely too heavily on notes or a manuscript.

Many speakers have been advised to stare over the heads of the audience at some mystical spot on the back wall of the auditorium. Not only does this ruin your chances of communicating to the listeners with your eyes, but it also prevents you from "reading" the responses of the audience.

Similarly, speakers are often told to pick someone in the audience to speak to. This is better, but be sure you don't turn your presentation into a limited engagement. Shift your eye contact about the room and try to connect with persons in every area.

AND IN YOUR FACE

Have you ever watched a conversation across a room, or behind a window? Seen a movie on an airplane without listening through the earphones? You don't really need to hear what is being said to gain some idea of the emotions of the participants. ("I can read your face like a book," we tell people—or the reaction to a look of contempt, "If looks could kill. . . .")

Remember that when you are speaking, your facial expressions are being examined. Don't let the pressures of making a presentation turn your visage to stone or to a silly, nervous smirk. Relax and be yourself. Show your best face to the audience.

Research has shown that when a person's words and facial expressions or gestures are inconsistent, the words are contradicted. In other words, "Watch what I do, not what I say." When someone says, "I believe you," with a forehead knit tightly in a sign of puzzlement, we don't really trust the statement. And what kind of message is sent if someone says "yes" but shakes his head from side to side in the recognized emblem meaning "no"?

And further, gum-chewing, smoking and drinking (except for an occasional sip of water if necessary) should not be part of your speaking repertoire. They are distractions which send messages of discourtesy and nervousness to the audience.

HANDING THE AUDIENCE A LINE

"What in the world do I do with my hands?" That has to be one of the most common concerns of the inexperienced (or ineffective) speaker.

The answer is, *use your hands and your body in a natural and spontaneous manner as part of your message delivery system.* Have someone study the way you use your hands in everyday conversation as part of your preparation for a speaking engagement or media appearance. It's okay to talk with your hands. It's expressive and attention-getting. *Additionally, the more you focus on your ideas, the more likely it is that your hands and arms will move* naturally *in response to the energy transmitted by your belief in what you're saying.* And remember ... speakers are far more prone to be "underanimated" than "overanimated." In fact, I can't remember the last "overanimated" executive I worked with.

What are some *unnatural* positions?

Leaning forward at the podium with your head supported on your arms.

Standing bolt upright with your hands clasped tightly behind your back (called the "reverse fig-leaf"), or with your arms folded tightly in front of your chest like a shield, or with your hands clasped tightly in front of your groin. (Yes, the "fig-leaf.")

Stuffing your hands into your pockets and leaving them there— sometimes adding music by playing with keys or loose change.

Any repetitive gestures that block the audience's view of your face (especially problematic for televised appearances).

Natural positions should require no definition. They are movements that do not draw attention to themselves but instead serve to illustrate or emphasize a message. They do not interfere with your delivery or make you appear or feel uncomfortable. A friend of mine who produces political commercials for television sometimes advises his less-than-animated clients to "make love" to their script, and yes, this graphic advice does produce results.

SPEAKING YOUR PIECE

Have you ever heard a talented speaker turn an indifferent text into a memorable presentation? Or a less endowed speaker ruin a marvelous piece of writing with a hemmed, hawed and slurred delivery?

Indeed, to a great extent the mode of your delivery greatly affects the reception of your message. It is important, then, to think about "voice," a critical *non-verbal* element of presentation.

There are five general dimensions of voice: *volume, rate, pitch, emphasis, and quality.*

Volume: This refers to the intensity of the voice used by the speaker. "Loudness" is a subjective evaluation of that volume, as affected by distance, acoustics and other noise. This is an area where most persons have developed an automatic regulating ability. Nonetheless, some people at an intimate cocktail party seem determined to yell as if they were at a Times Square subway stop at rush hour with four trains pulling in. And, of course, some choose to whisper in a packed auditorium.

We need to reinforce our skills—to fine-tune our antennae—to estimate approximately how much volume is needed to communicate in a particular setting.

It is, however, important to add a few refinements to your volume-setting ability—the use of varying levels of volume to keep the voice interesting to the listener and to *emphasize* words or phrases. It is a very common and problematic practice to allow the voice to fade off at the end of sentences, particularly at the end of ideas and at the end of the presentation, almost as if the speaker were collapsing at the end of a race.

Rate: Here is another area of difficulty for many persons. Assuming you are able to speak clearly, the most common problems are speaking more slowly than necessary and speaking too quickly toward the latter quarter of a prepared presentation. A typical recommended rate of speed is between 130 and 170 words per minute. Tape record one of your practice sessions and check a section against a watch. As noted earlier, experts say that the mind of the listener can typically accept as much as three to four times as many words per minute as a speaker can deliver.

Of course, the pace of your delivery should vary depending upon the nature of your message, and should also vary within the presentation to offer variety to the listener. Generally, serious material is delivered a bit more slowly, humor a bit more quickly. A formal setting, or one before a very large gathering with a great deal of distance between you and the audience, would probably justify a slower, more deliberative presentation; a small, informal circle might require a quicker pace.

Pitch: This is the measurement of "highness" or "lowness" of voice. As in volume and rate, it is something you should learn to change for emphasis, meaning and variety.

We often assign greater authority to a speaker—male or female—who uses a low to moderate range of voice. For examples, look to the professional news readers on television.

Because pitch is to a large part determined by the tension or relaxation of the vocal cords, many speakers find their voices are at a higher pitch when they are under pressure—for example, when making a presentation. Relaxation is the cure, and that is something that comes with practice and experience. It should not be your goal to alter your voice, though—just to be able to use it in a normal tone.

Emphasis: This is a most significant element of our non-verbal communication. A change in emphasis greatly alters meaning; read out loud the following sentence, emphasizing the italicized words:

What do you want me to do? (anger)
What *do* you want me to do? (querulousness)
What do *you* want me to do? (as opposed to what *he* wants you to do)
What do you *want* me to do? (what you *really* want)
What do you want *me* to do? (as opposed to *him*)
What do you want me to *do*? (a plaintive plea)

Quality: Quality of voice is a subjective matter, as determined by the listener. This includes elements such as "breathiness," "hoarseness," nasality and other qualities. Listen to a good-quality tape recording of your voice. Seek open feedback from others.

Also included here are some "speech defects," including slurring of words, problems with particular speech sounds and chronic mispronunciation of certain common words—"revelant" for "relevant,""li-berry" for "library," "ag-cul-ture" for agriculture and perhaps the most common one we experience in our seminars, "nu-cu-lar" for "nuclear." You may find you have a habit of adding sounds ("judg-ah-ment"), or dropping sounds (goin', doin').

THE PAUSES THAT REFLECT

Part of your non-verbal speech are the "pauses" we need to insert. Professor Mark Knapp of Purdue calls these "unfilled" or silent pauses, and "filled" pauses.

The unfilled pauses have been shown to add to the perception of the speaker's credibility and the depth of preparation. Specifically, it appears to the listener to be an example of the speaker thinking carefully about what he or she wants to say. Pauses also serve as part of the punctuation of your presentation and as reinforcement of feeling—for instance, a heartfelt pause conveys great sadness or respect.

Despite these obvious benefits of pauses, speakers normally *overreact* to the temporary silence associated with them. Rather than focusing on the merits of pausing deliberately to promote audience comprehension and the speaker's relaxation, speakers become all too concerned about appearing forgetful or, worse yet, stupid.

Most speakers do need to pay some attention to the filled pauses, the *vocalizers* they may be inserting, "you know," in your, "uhh," speech. Vocalizers are often unconscious nervous habits, aimed at avoiding at all costs a pause of silence. They are not easy to get rid of, but the first step is to train yourself to become aware of them. Conscientious practice plus a tape recorder and trusted friend can help you keep score.

CHAPTER **3**

Well Dressed Is Best

Initially, one might be understandably skeptical or somewhat defensive about following detailed advice regarding how to dress. But if you do have what it takes to be successful and you don't know how to dress, you're like a product on the market without a package—or at least without an appealing one.

Being well dressed is critical to your image as a communicator; it can communicate authority, pride, success and other traits which help transmit and reinforce your credibility.

Being well dressed can make you feel better—offer you added confidence which can help you alleviate any nervous tension associated with a presentation, speaking engagement or media appearance.

Granted, different professions and situations cause one to define "well dressed" differently, but the following advice is normally appropriate for the more typical executive and his environment.*

FOR THE BUSINESSMAN

The suit: Since the business suit is the staple of a professional man's attire, a great deal of attention should be devoted to its

---

*Much of the advice that follows is based on John T. Molloy's *Dress for Success*, Warner Books, New York, 1975, and from our association with Karen Kaufmann, a Philadelphia-based image consultant.

selection and fit. Styling should be conservative and traditional—never too sharply fitted or adorned with flashy ornamentation such as extra buttons, fancy stitching or patches. The single-breasted suit is best, except perhaps for tall, thin men who might look better in a double-breasted style.

Vests project a "corporate image" of formality, and should be worn only where that is an appropriate image. Further, vests have a tendency to bunch under a jacket, retain body heat and add too much bulk to medium and large-framed men.

A proper fitting is imperative. Clothes should be altered so they won't bulge, wrinkle or show gaps. Pants without a cuff should break in the front and be one-half to three-quarters of an inch longer in the back. Pants *with* cuffs should hang horizontal to the ground.

To judge the proper length of a jacket, stand with arms flat and curl the fingers so that the jacket fits into the curl. The sleeve should rest about five inches above the tip of the thumb, leaving one-half inch of the shirt visible.

The recommended fabric for shirts is the wash-and-wear blend of cotton and polyester. Knits are generally too warm and subject to snags. As with a suit, fit is very important. There should be no pulling around the buttons, and the shirt should be long enough to stay tucked into the pants in normal activities.

What color is your "white" shirt? The shirt should always be lighter than the suit, and the tie darker than the shirt.

The recommended colors for business suits are shades of blue, gray and beige. Brown and black are usually inappropriate. The basic dark solid suit is fine; also acceptable are pinstripes (white stripes deemed most sophisticated) and subtle plaids.

Research indicates that basic white or pale blue are best for shirts. Also good are pastels; subtle, lighter shades are more evocative of the executive image. Solid oxford cloths are highly thought of, followed by thin, single-color stripes. The only other acceptable pattern, according to the experts, is a simple, delicate box plaid. Dots, floral designs and paisley, as well as all short-sleeve shirts, are too sporty for the office. Pleats, fancy yokes or epaulets are also inappropriate.

A business shirt should not have more than one simple flap pocket; some of the most formal shirts have none.

The tie that binds: Though it is the smallest element of a suit, the tie is probably the most important element in terms of status, since it projects respectability and professionalism.

The best ties are silk or polyester and silk blends. The solid-color tie is a sensible complement to any outfit. Small polka dots, with the dot picking up the color of the suit and the background contrasting, are elegant. Other patterns are the classic "club" tie which carries the emblem of a "class" sport such as sailing, the diagonally striped "rep" tie, or the "Ivy League" pattern of small circles or diamonds. Conservative paisley and plaid designs are acceptable when they accent a subtle suit. Large or gaudy patterns, or bow ties, are not recommended.

The length of the tie should be such that it lightly sweeps the belt buckle. Its width should be harmonious with the width of the suit's lapels—this is one area where man's fashion follows cycles of design.

THE "TOTAL" LOOK

Small-framed men should wear high-authority clothing, such as pinstriped suits and shirts, Ivy League ties and vests. Larger men should avoid dark suits and pinstripes and opt for softer colors and textures.

Pay some attention to the education, occupation and status of each day's clients in choosing your most successful outfit.

Accessories: Wingtip and lace shoes in black, brown and cordovan are best. Slip-ons are acceptable if very plain. Cowboy boots are for cowboys. Socks should be dark and worn over the calf.

Perhaps the two most important accessories in terms of image are a pen and an attaché case. A thin silver or gold pen or pencil is a sure sign of prestige. Image consultants also advise a business professional always to carry an attaché case—even if it merely contains the morning newspaper.

A wedding band is acceptable, as are small and elegant tie pins and clasps. Thin, plain gold watches are appropriate. Any other items of jewelry, including ID bracelets, collar pins or neck chains, are not recommended.

Wire-frame eyeglasses project a younger image; heavy horn-rimmed frames give an older appearance. The frame should accent hair color.

There is no hard-and-fast rule on hair length, other than the recommendation that hair be neat and well-trimmed. Facial hair of any type is not recommended, except to compensate for a weakness in appearance.

The traditional raincoat should be beige. Overcoats should also be in a camel color with tailored lines. Gloves are best in rich brown.

A final note on accessories: wallets should be a dark, rich brown or cordovan color, and the longer "pocket secretary" is a status symbol in comparison to the typical hip pocket billfold. Wallets should never bulge or contain an accumulation of unnecessary items that are obvious when taken out in public. Handkerchiefs showing from the left breast pocket—generally an accessory for older men—should be white.

FOR THE FEMALE EXECUTIVE

Fashion consultants advise that female executives acknowledge that fashion and femininity are inappropriate in the office. At the same time, women must guard against projecting too masculine an image. Therefore, a conservative wardrobe that will win respect rather than admiration belongs in the closet of the successful businesswoman.

The "skirted suit": The female equivalent of the man's business suit is a matching skirted suit.

The cut of the suit should be full and not designed to exaggerate the figure. The traditionally designed man-tailored jacket is best. Skirts should look comfortable, not confining; and their length should be just below the knee. Vests are also too great a concession to fashion, and should be avoided since their tight fit accentuates the bust line, especially when worn without a jacket. As with men, vests are usually only suggested for small-framed women.

Exotic colors and extremely bright shades of color should be avoided. As with the male's wardrobe, colors in the blue, gray and beige families are most appropriate.

The best material for a suit is wool or linen. Solids, tasteful tweeds and delicate plaids are acceptable patterns. However, pin-stripes should be avoided, since that projects a masculine image.

Blouses: A blouse is for women what a tie is for men—the item that makes a bold difference in an outfit, coordinating the total look. To remain within executive lines, the blouse should be simply styled and not overly dressy, frilly or full of lace. Collars may be worn inside or outside the suit jacket. Necklines should be carefully selected so that the opening is equivalent to a man's shirt with one button open.

Solid blouses are the easiest to coordinate, yet any simple, non-frilly pattern is acceptable. Suggested colors range from white to black, excepting only flashy colors and overly feminine pastels. Sheer blouses should be avoided and a camisole or full slip should be worn to camouflage bra lines.

COORDINATING THE LOOK

It is difficult to generalize about women's clothing because there are so many styles, patterns and colors available. Some guide-lines, though:

First, creating a sense of presence and authority is imperative, especially since many women are small-framed. Here, color is particularly important. For example, a gray suit with a traditional white blouse projects presence and authority. Yet a gray suit with a black blouse may overemphasize authority.

Second, while trying to compensate for a small frame through dress, a woman may seem *too* harsh, especially to other women. Adding some softer colors for blouses may help in building trust and believability.

Third, a woman at work doesn't need a huge collection of suits and blouses. Instead, as with men, she needs a handful of basic suits that can be interchanged to create a wardrobe.

Accessories: Closed-toe pumps with $1^1/_2$-inch heels are the acceptable business shoes for women. A simply styled pair in blue, black, beige, gray and deep maroon should assure a set to match every outfit.

Stockings should be skin-colored and an extra pair should be stored in a desk drawer and glove compartment to deal with embarrassing runs.

A pen and pencil, preferably gold, and a briefcase are essential items for women, too. The briefcase should serve as a handbag as well. If needed, a handbag should be small and uncluttered. The most useful piece of jewelry for women is a wedding ring—some women wear one even if not married. It helps to keep relationships on a business basis. Any other jewelry should be simple and functional—a traditional watch, rings in a low setting (never more than one on each hand) and post earrings.

The best makeup is unobtrusive. Heavy eyeshadow or eyeliner is obtrusive. Nails and cuticles should be well-trimmed and short; clear nail polish is best.

Hair styling should also be subtle. Medium-length hair is best, with styles that do not need constant attention a plus. Hair color should not be tipped or streaked, and some natural gray adds a sense of maturity.

Moderate-size eyeglasses add authority. Frames should be bone or plastic, preferably brown. Designer frames and wire-rims are not appropriate.

The best coats are camel color in a double-breasted, notch-collar style. Like the suit jacket, the coat should not outline the figure too tightly. Fur collars are best held for evening wear. Gloves—not mittens—should be deep black, brown or maroon leather.

One other accessory for the female executive is a credit card. It is the accepted way to pay for lunches and dinners, and can be left on the table as a subtle signal to the waiter not to place the bill in front of a male guest.

CHAPTER **4**

Using Language—How to Say What You Mean

If your speech reads well, it is probably not a good one. Oral and written language are two very different forms of communication. What succeeds in print may very well flop when spoken; what sounds powerful and convincing when spoken may look weak and pointless on paper.

Furthermore, your message is a fleeting communication.

- The audience cannot stop and reread an orally presented paragraph to help comprehend a message—or to pick up the thread if there has been an interruption. There is no opportunity for the listener to run to a dictionary or to a reference book if you use an unfamiliar word or term.

- Moreover, it is difficult to retract the spoken word. There is very little time between the development of a thought and the moment you speak it; the editing and revising process that comes between the first and the final version of a written presentation just doesn't exist.

- And perhaps most important, oral language itself is different from the written word. We'll discuss those important distinctions soon.

But don't think that written communication has all the advantages; in fact, oral language may even represent the trump card. Oral presentation has the power of projecting greater personal involvement. A speaker can employ a multitude of persuasive techniques that are beyond the one-dimensional written word.

So, too, a speaker has the tremendous advantage of being able to "read" his audience. He can adjust his message or his delivery based on the response he receives as he is speaking. He can also open the floor to questions to clarify or to reinforce his message, or he can move into other areas of interest and, as a consequence, add to the persuasiveness of the message.

TOWARD MORE VIVID SPEECH

"What did you have for lunch?"
"A hamburger on a bun."
"Oh, that's nice."
"What did **you** have for lunch?"
"It was a charcoal-broiled, medium-rare ground beef patty, bubbling with flavor, on a toasted sesame roll with a perfect slice of red Bermuda onion, a dollop of ketchup and a kosher dill pickle on the side."
"You're making me hungry just hearing you talk about it. Tell me more!"

Oral language offers you the opportunity to use words in their most vivid, evocative forms. And if you have any remaining doubt about the effectiveness of picturesque language in a persuasive presentation, consider this:*

Researchers E.F. Loftus and J.C. Palmer showed a fascinating link between language and mental imagery in their studies of a group of subjects who were asked questions about an automobile collision. Different persons were given different stories about the accident: some were told the cars had "smashed"; others heard that the vehicles had "collided," "bumped," "hit" or "contacted."

The subjects all saw the same film of an accident and were then asked to estimate the speed of the cars. The difference between those told of a "smash" and those told of "contact" was nine miles per hour—no matter that they saw the same accident in the film.

---

*E.F. Loftus and J.C. Palmer, "Reconstruction of Automobile Destruction: An Example of the Interaction between Language and Memory," *Journal of Verbal Learning and Verbal Behavior 13* (1974): 585–589.

The results with average speed:

Smashed—40.8 mph
Collided—39.3 mph
Bumped—38.1 mph
Hit—34.0 mph
Contacted—31.8 mph

Although there was no broken glass evident in the film shown to the subjects, 32 percent of those who were told of a "smash" reported seeing broken glass, while only 14 percent of those who were told the cars "hit" had the same memory.

All this for the selection of a single verb!

Picturesque speech aside, oral presentations have other characteristics, including:

Shorter words and phrases.
Use of fragmentary sentences.
Asides, parenthetical remarks and other interruptions to the linear flow of a presentation.
Increased use of personal pronouns. "I am" and "you are" and "we do" all work to draw your listeners into your message.
Less formal construction, including use of contractions (can't, won't, we're).
Use of slang and colloquialisms. This, however, does not excuse language that is improper or unsuited to the time or occasion.
Regular use of internal summaries, restatement and signposts for the listener.
Rhetorical devices to involve the audience. Asking questions of specific individuals or merely posing them to the group at large are among such devices. Remember Ronald Reagan's compelling questions at the end of his presidential debate in 1980 with Jimmy Carter: "Are you better off than you were four years ago?"
The use of rhetorical devices to make a point. Rhythm and construction can add to your delivery and to the persuasiveness of your message.

What are the language requirements for an oral presentation?

1. It must be easily and quickly understood, without each point overlapping into the time required for the next. Therefore, the message must be stated very directly.
2. There must be sufficient restatement to tie up the points in a neat package for the listener.
3. The message must be easily—and comfortably—spoken.

Because the listener cannot jump back a page to reread a statement, or pause for research or consultation, the burden is upon the speaker to be clear and specific. The two principal enemies of clarity are vagueness and ambiguity.

Vagueness is the failure of the speaker to illuminate abstract or general concepts with specific examples or facts. No clear meaning emerges from a statement.

> *Vague:* "Our lives depend upon a certain amount of trust of our fellow man. We have to hope that our neighbors will always follow the rules and the expectations of society."

> *Specific:* "Our lives depend upon a certain amount of trust of our fellow man. We buy our over-the-counter drugs and we have to trust that no one has poisoned them, as happened in 1982 with the Tylenol killings. We pass in our car through an intersection and rely on our faith that the driver approaching from the other direction will stop at the red light. That didn't happen here in Maple Grove last week in that tragic accident on Main Street."

To use E.B. White's well-known dictum on specificity: "Don't talk about *man*, talk about *a man*."

Ambiguity arises when there is more than one possible meaning from any element of a presentation—any word or phrase.

> "John told Harry that he had been fired." Who was fired? John or Harry?

> Groucho Marx: "When I was on safari in Africa, I shot an elephant in my pajamas. (How he got in my pajamas I'll never know.)"

DEVELOPING YOUR STYLE

It is probably safe to say that if something can be defined as "having style," chances are it doesn't. Style is that ephemeral element that lifts a phrase, a thought, a proposal from background noise to sudden piercing clarity, vitality, and memorability. It is easier to define by its absence than by its presence.

Style is a personal matter. You are unique, and your words will be unlike anyone else's if you let them be. The key is to combine that uniqueness with effectiveness.

Here are some specific examples of non-stylishness:

Wordiness and round-about phrasing: It's worth a mild chuckle to speak of a trash collector as a "sanitary engineer" or a "garbologist" or of a fire alarm as a "combustion enunciator." But if you're not looking for weak humor, avoid such circumlocutions. Government and the military, of course, are chockablock with such titles; your presentations should not be. "Once we interface with the proper authorities, we're going to extend our ETA slightly to allow the airframe inspection consortium to minimize the capability deficiencies," the Air Force spokesman said. What he meant was, "We will try to fix the plane before we take off, and so we'll be a little late."

Mouthing the trite: If a phrase springs immediately to mind, it is probably a cliché. Many such phrases are so tired from overuse that the mind automatically tunes them out. If you go to the well too often, your cup may not runneth over but instead may be as dry as the Sahara sands.

Unnecessary complexity of language: Don't use words like *"circumlocution"* and *"chockablock"* unless you are pretty sure you and your audience understand their meanings. Uncommon words can add to the coloration of your presentation, but they can also bewilder, confuse and lead the audience away from your message. Are you trying to impress the audience or to persuade them? Is your ego running interference with your ideas?

Euphemisms: Euphemisms are all too frequently the enemy of clarity. "Advancing toward the rear" may sound less like a defeat than "retreat," but "retreat" means the same and it says it more directly, which should be your aim. Leave the propagandizing to others.

The passive voice: A favorite of the bureaucrat, it takes the energy out of a statement, which may be a good defensive move, but it communicates poorly. "Coinciding with the implementation of rationing was the appearance of an extensive unofficial private market." OR: "The black market arrived soon after rationing began."

Unnecessary flourishes: The author of *Hamlet* may well be referred to by some as the "Bard of Stratford-upon-Avon," but why not call him "William Shakespeare" to your audience? Show you care by saying it *without* flowers.

Here are some things to do to make your language and your presentations more colorful and understandable:

1. Speak the language of your listeners. Avoid technical jargon and acronyms. They don't express or impress, but they can distress.
2. When you must use a technical term, define it immediately in the simplest terms possible.
3. Be aware of multiple meanings and homonyms. "I went to the nudist colony, but it was more than I could bear." (Think about it—your audience would.)
4. Think in graphic terms—words that stimulate pictures in your listeners' minds. "Have you ever felt the power of the escaping steam through the pouring spout of your teapot? Well, a steam locomotive is like a teapot on wheels."

UNDER CONSTRUCTION: VIVID, CLEAR SPEECH

One of your most important tasks as a speaker is to define your terms and make your message clear.

You can define by using a *synonym*, being careful not to substitute one ambiguous term for another. You can define by *example*, using a situation or historical event known to your audience. You can define by *comparison* or *contrast*, explaining what something is like and unlike. You can define by *negation*, explaining what a particular word is not. You can define by *etymology*, giving an explanation of the origin of a term or how it has evolved from one meaning to its present status. And, you can define by *detail* or *operation*, explaining a concept by showing how it works.

And probably best of all, you can and should make yourself clear by combining many different types of definitions, including definition by exposition—a visual aid, whether it be an object, such as a model, a chart, a diagram or a photograph.

SOME TOOLS OF THE TRADE

Like a good backyard mechanic, it pays to have the right tools sitting around waiting for just the right moment. You can make your presentations come alive by using the following devices:

Simile: "I feel like something the dog dragged in." A simile relates two seemingly dissimilar ideas or objects with "like," "as" or "as if."

Metaphor: Researching a speech can be "a hard row to hoe." There is no qualifying "like" to a metaphor—one object or idea *is* another object or idea, you are saying. "I am a dog among the sheep."

A clumsy pass at use of metaphor, though, can give your audience some unexpected opportunities to laugh—at you and not with you. "While this is only the latest storm to engulf us, there have been many other detours along the road."

The New Yorker magazine specializes in running examples of failed metaphors and other egregious language.

BLOCK THAT METAPHOR!*

If Henry Knowles is making life more difficult for the industry, so are the times. It has had to adjust to the new rules through mercurial fluctuations in the economic temperature—from the steamy, amorous heat of takeover fever, to the passion-sapping chill of recession in which the tumescent lust of so many of the market's big shooters has shrivelled into flaccid impotence as they find themselves enmeshed in corporate paternity suits they can no longer afford.

Hyperbole: This is intentional exaggeration or overstatement. "The whole world is watching."

Understatement: The opposite of hyperbole, it can be even more effective, assuming the audience understands the fact that you are using the device. "Babe Ruth was known to make contact with the ball every now and then," or, to a good-natured and sodden audience after a week of steady rain, "I understand it's been a little damp here lately."

Antithesis: By this is meant a parallel construction with opposing parts. The rich and the poor, the educated and the undereducated will appreciate the message this program brings."

Antimetabole: The juxtaposition of the same words in successive phrases; "The pessimist sees the difficulty in every opportunity; the optimist, the opportunity in every difficulty."**

---

*The New Yorker Magazine, Inc., New York, Sept. 27, 1982, Page 133.
**L.P. Jacks, 1860–1955, English philosopher and clergyman.

Personification: This means the assignment of human-like qualities to an object or idea. The description of the Watergate events as a "cancer on the presidency" is one example. We say that "luck smiles" and "fate frowns" and "destiny beckons"—and so do tiresome clichés, so be forewarned.

Rhetorical questions: Asking yourself a question is often a good way to introduce a new subject. Asking the question of the audience is often a good way to involve them in your presentation. The danger, though, is that someone might respond to your question out loud with an answer unsuited to your purpose in posing the question. (More discussion in Question-and-Answer Sessions in Chapter 12.)

THE POETRY OF SPOKEN WORDS

A good portion of the power of a spoken presentation comes from the sound of the words. We'll discuss some of the techniques you can use to enhance your delivery in a later chapter, but for now, consider some aural effects of an oral presentation:

Alliteration: The repetition of a consonant sound, for example, "The hallowed halls of Harvard" or, from Winston Churchill, a past master:

> "The Battle of Britain is about to begin.... Let us therefore brace ourselves to our duty and so bear ourselves that if the British Commonwealth and Empire last for a thousand years, men will still say, "This was their finest hour."*

Assonance: The repetition of the same stressed vowel sound. "Four score," from Lincoln's "Gettysburg Address."

Repetition: "I have a dream," said Martin Luther King. "A dream...."

Parallelism: The use of words in a pattern, a rhythm like music and poetry. "We are fully prepared; we are fully committed; we await the signal to begin." There is an added benefit here: in addition to the appeal of the rhythmic presentation, by interspersing short sentences with longer ones and allowing for dramatic pause, you will

---

*Winston Churchill, House of Commons speech, June 18, 1940.

also be buying breathing spaces for yourself, thereby aiding your delivery.

Onomatopoeia and sound suggestion: "Crash!" sounds like a crash; "boom!" sounds like a boom. Words with onomatopoetic qualities can conjure up sound images in the minds of your listeners. Sound suggestion is the assignment of an image by use of a word: to call someone a jerk is more than to claim that the person is a fool. The word includes a harsh judgment in its sound.

TRIPPING OVER YOUR TONGUE

Just as your audience can hear without listening, so too, it can listen without receiving a correct message. Some words with very different meanings sound alike; some words mean different things in different contexts; some words gain different senses because of conscious or unconscious signals from the speaker.

Semanticists say there are three principal ways by which we perceive a meaning: *denotation, connotation* and *context.*

Denotation: The literal relationship between a word and the object it stands for. We speakers of English have all agreed that a sheaf of papers bound between covers is called a book. The word "book" denotes that object.

Connotation: The relationship between the word, the object it represents, and the speaker and/or listener. Using the word "book" before an audience of authors or booksellers or literary critics connotes a personal, involved definition. Using the word "hippie" at an American Legion hall carries a certain connotation which might not be registered with an audience of college students.

Context: Most of our communication is not made up of single words. "Book" has a meaning, but a sentence made up of just that one word has no meaning by itself, unless it is answering a question or is accompanied by an expressive non-verbal gesture.

The *structural context* of a sentence also conveys meaning through use of signals. Consider the following: "My dog howls at the moon." "My" identifies the noun. It could have been *your* dog; it could have been *his* dog; it might have been *the* dog, referring to a specific animal, or it could have been *a* dog, which is non-specific. There is only one "dog"; dogs would have told us there were at least two. My dog *"howls"* at the moon, which means that the howling is presently going on. My dog could have *howled*; I could say he *will howl* at some future time.

The relationship between words can give a sentence many different meanings. Consider:

Mommy said, "Tommy, the turtle is dead." The mother is informing Tommy that the turtle is deceased.

"Mommy," said Tommy, "the turtle is dead." Tommy is informing Mommy that the turtle is no longer alive.

Mommy said, "Tommy the turtle is dead." In which Mommy informs the world that a turtle by the name of Tommy has breathed his last breath.

"Mommy," said Tommy the turtle, "is dead." That's right— it's the turtle named Tommy, informing us that Mommy has departed this earthly vale.

The relationship between words here is apparent to the careful reader because of the use of punctuation marks. There are no such written devices available to the speaker; you must find a way to be clear and unambiguous without them.

SOUNDS GRATE

Sometimes the meaning of our words depends upon the accent we apply to their syllables.

The *com*-plex of rooms that makes up the City Council follows a very com-*plex* design; you will only com-*pound* your troubles if you fail to follow the map of the *com*-pound.

And at times the words look alike and are sounded alike.

If you lose your belongings on your way out of the *council*, you might want to seek the *counsel* of a *counsel*. (Unless you feel that they meant to *desert* you as a just *dessert*.)

Differences in meaning can also arise from the emphasis given certain words within a sentence:

I can go anywhere I please.
I can *go* anywhere I please.
I can go *anywhere* I please.
I can go anywhere *I* please.
I can go anywhere I *please*.

PART 2

Speeches and Presentations

CHAPTER 5

Speaking with a Purpose—Set Your Goals First

Why do you want to speak?

> To inform?
> To convince?
> To persuade?
> To inspire?
> To entertain?

Why would an audience want to listen?

> Your credibility?
> Your authority?
> Your personal involvement?
> Their self-interest?

What will you talk about?

> An assigned topic?
> A topic of your choosing?

Is the topic appropriate?

> To you?
> To your audience?
> To the setting and time?

IMAGE AND SUBSTANCE GOALS

Very often speakers will merely choose a subject they think will be interesting to the audience, rather than identifying particular image and substance goals. Indeed, executives would be well advised to define the traits they should project (image goals), the ideas they should present, and the attitudes they need to modify (substance goals).

One of my clients, a nationally known political figure, confessed that he had never before sat down to define the goals of his speech. He had merely assembled the elements he thought his audience wanted to hear. He was the first to admit that his speeches were often terribly disorganized. As soon as he began defining the image and substance goals of his presentations, he became more comfortable with his assignments, and, predictably, more effective.

THE IMPORTANCE OF IMAGE

Regardless of an executive's competence or power, a significant portion of his or her ability to persuade is related to image. Image is projected in countless ways—your manner of dress, type of car, location and furnishings of an office, as well as how others perceive your family life, truthfulness, interest in others, decisiveness and dynamism. However, many executives are unwilling or unable to come to terms with their self-image and related speech anxiety.

Monitoring your image should be part of your management system. Consider developing an "Image Profile" of yourself, a detailed inventory of the major traits—positive and negative—you project. To accomplish this, you should work with a few close confidants or with an executive communication consultant—or preferably with both.

Many executives are reluctant to seek candid, constructive feedback, or to express their feelings openly. At the same time, some of their closest colleagues may be reluctant to offer the type of feedback needed.

One solution is to develop a feedback system:

- Don't wait for feedback; be prepared to ask for it.

- Seek out one-on-one sessions with trusted colleagues.

- Ask specific questions, making it clear you are seeking information for your self-development, and not for an ego massage.
- Encourage others to approach you if they have constructive information for you.
- Conduct periodic meetings aimed at gleaning general impressions on how you are perceived by the people inside and outside your organization.
- Listen well, question intently, guard against any hint of defensiveness, and show appreciation for the candor expressed by your colleagues.

The most significant dimension of the Image Profile will be your credibility. Most research identifies these four components of credibility:

1. *Competence:* Your qualifications to perform, intelligence, sensibility, achievements, ability to communicate;
2. *Safety:* Your projection of good will, interest in others, and compassion;
3 *Character:* Your honesty, candor, soundness of values and record of promises kept; and
4. *Dynamism:* Your energy, depth of conviction, self-confidence and orientation toward action.

Once the Image Profile has been compiled, you should devote your attention to an Executive Image Strategic Plan that will strengthen the perception of some traits and maintain others. Obviously, you shouldn't undertake major changes in your behavior or personality if you are not comfortable doing so. And, of course, the changes should not be so obvious as to draw skepticism or backlash from your audience.

After you've developed an Image Profile and Strategic Plan, you should designate what particular image goals should be sought from a particular engagement. Do you want to project personal and corporate compassion or concern? Resolve? Creativity? Your audience analysis, which will be discussed later, will help you to refine your image goals.

Decide what range of topics will help you reinforce your image goals before a particular audience (that is, if you and not the host organization have retained control of the topic).

SUBSTANCE GOALS

What messages do you need to convey to your internal and external audiences? That you care about your employees? That despite recent economic downturns, there is realistic hope for your company's progress? That your rates are reasonable? That you truly care about the community? About the environment?

Choosing a topic of common interest to you and your audience is critical to fulfilling your substance goals and helps induce in the audience a "need to know" or "need to listen." It is also very important in preparing your own mindset for speaking. If the topic is interesting to you and not to the audience, you're choosing a very difficult if not impossible objective. If the subject is interesting to the audience but not to you, you're starting out with two strikes against you.

Most presentations are, believe it or not, largely persuasive— that is, they seek to modify the audience's attitudes or behavior towards the speaker, the ideas presented, and, of course, the company. Crucial, then, to effective persuasion is effective audience analysis—knowing where your audience stands so you can change its position, if only by small degrees.

CHAPTER **6**

Why Are We Here? Advance Work and Audience Analysis

You are now planning a speech to accomplish important image and substance goals. What's the audience's reason for attending?

- Are they *coerced*—there because they have to be there? Is it a condition of employment that they attend a session with their supervisor or boss? Are they students forced to attend a lecture? Are members of the audience attending out of social necessity—as much to be seen as to hear?

- Is the audience there because it wants to hear someone other than you?

- Is the audience in *voluntary* attendance—there of its own free will because of a genuine interest in you and your message? Don't assume, though, that a voluntary audience will be friendly. Hecklers and picketers can be voluntary attendees as well.

- Is the audience made up of an *organization* gathered because of a common interest or background?

ADVANCING YOUR PRESENTATION

One of the more critical elements of any operation—political, military, social, business or otherwise—is the gathering of intelligence. Small problems are much more easily dealt with while they are small; programs are much easier to change before they are printed and bound.

In the political world, the person who performs this task is called the "advance man." It is his or her job to travel ahead of the candidate and choose locations for speeches, make reservations for rooms, arrange for any special needs of the speaker, drum up interest among the media, put out brush fires among the locals and prepare a meticulous schedule of the politician's movements—almost moment by moment and step by step.

You, too, need an advance man, even if you do the work yourself. In a word, the more you are aware of what to expect, the more confident you should be—and the less you should be preoccupied with a fear of the unknown. Moreover, this awareness can allow you to determine your latitude of control over your speaking environment: *the greater your latitude of control, the greater your persuasive potential.*

You might consider this section of the chapter a checklist.

Well before you walk into a room to make a presentation, you should know as much as you can about the *audience* and the occasion.

1. How many people are expected?
2. Who are they? The male:female ratio? Educational level? Age breakdown? Economic status? Political preferences? etc.
3. Why are they there?
4. Is there anyone in attendance whom you know, or who has a special relationship with or knowledge of you?
5. What is the nature of the event? A regular or special meeting? Of how much importance is it regarded by those expected to attend?

You should know all you can about the *group*:

1. What are the common interests of its members?
2. What are their attitudes about you, your company, and your topic?
3. How informed are they about the subject of your speech?
4. What do they expect to hear from you?
5. Who else have they heard speak recently?

You need to know about the day's *schedule*:

1. Where are you in terms of the full day's schedule?
2. Are you the only speaker? If not, who will precede you and who will follow you? What will they talk about?

3. Will you be seated at the head table?
4. Who will be seated near you? What are their backgrounds?
5. Will a meal be served before you speak?
6. Will the dishes have been cleared?
7. What type of dress is expected?
8. When are you expected to begin?
9. When are you expected to finish?
10. Will you be expected to answer questions from the audience? If so, who will recognize questioners from the audience? Will you have the assistance of a moderator to cut off hostile or troublesome questioners? Who will end the session?
11. Have the media been notified of your appearance?
12. Do the hosts expect television crews? Will they tape during your presentation or seek an interview afterwards? Or do both?

You should be fully briefed on the *physical arrangements*:

1. How large a room? (The best advance men try to arrange for a room which is just slightly too small for the occasion—they figure it looks better to have 500 persons in a room seating 475 than 500 in a room seating 1,000. Don't go overboard, though, for you run the risk of alienating your audience.)
2. What will be the seating arrangements? Rows? Round tables? U-shaped tables?
3. Will you be speaking from a platform? Will there be a podium? Can it be adjusted to the proper height? Is there room on the podium for your notes? Does it have a lip on the bottom to prevent your notes from falling to the floor? Is it wide enough to accommodate two short piles of notes—those used and those to be used? Is there a light on the podium? Controls for audio-visual equipment?
4. Will you require a microphone? Where will the microphone be mounted? Are lavalier or wireless microphones available?
5. What kind of lighting will be used? How controllable is it?
6. Is the room set up to accommodate projectors or other electric devices for visual aids? Do you need to bring your own projector, tape recorder or other devices? If you will use equipment in place, are you certain it is compatible with the films, slides or tapes you will bring? Is a stock of electrical cords, light bulbs and fuses available? Is a screen available? Can it be seen from all parts of the room? Will you need a projectionist?

You should know about your *entrance and exit*:

1. Who will greet you when you arrive? Are there any special events before or after your presentation? Will you come onto the stage from the wings or from the floor?
2. Who will introduce you? What will he say? Have you provided current information about you and your company? Is there anything special you would like him to say?
3. How will you get off the stage? Can you arrange for the host or moderator to assist you in ending your presentation if you have a particular schedule to follow?
4. Is there an office available for your use before or after your presentation? Is there a telephone number you can obtain in advance to leave with your own office for emergencies?

What can you learn from the demographic and attitudinal information gleaned as a result of the advance work? For instance, how does speaking to an all-male audience affect your presentation? What about a senior citizens group as opposed to the Jaycees? The ASPCA or the National Rifle Association?

Sex: There is probably nothing that can be assumed anymore in terms of sex roles in our society. All women are not housewives staying home watching the soap operas and all men are not macho breadwinners who make all of the family's economic and political decisions.

We do know that males and females respond differently to the same message. Appeals that are likely to persuade women fall flat when tried with men.

Some studies imply that men tend to be swayed more by appeals of reason, while women react more readily to arguments based on emotion. At the same time, women have been shown to retain more specific details of an argument than do men.

Age: Experience, cultural surroundings and upbringing make for significant differences in the responses of older audiences as compared to those of younger ones. Researchers say that young persons are more likely to accept proposals for change, while an older audience might rely instead on its sense of perspective. This type of research, by the way, substantiates theories dating back to Aristotle (384–322 B.C.), who said that youth was radical, idealistic and willing to change. The old, Aristotle said, are not easily excited, and they weigh all the facts and make their decisions based on experience. The middle-aged, he said, don't hold strong opinions on anything.

Older audiences have also been shown to prefer a slower, more deliberate pace of speaking. Younger persons, perhaps because they are the children of the television age, seem to prefer quicker, more visual presentations.

Social or economic status: A group of factory workers carries different educational and economic backgrounds than does a group of university professors. Inner-city residents have different bases of experience than do rural or farm populations.

Don't assume, by the way, that a better-educated group will necessarily be more receptive to your message. Sociologists speak of a person's background and experience in terms of a triangle, with opinion at the topmost tip. For a person with a great deal of experience, the base of the triangle may be so broad as to make the tip very narrow; therefore he may be much less persuadable.

Religion: Just as with sex, there are no longer many absolutes left. It is not possible to make hard-and-fast predictions on moral and ethical positions, but it is still worthwhile to consider religious background in designing the tone and nature of your message. A speech about birth control before a Catholic audience would have to be delicately phrased; so, too, a Middle East policy analysis before a Jewish group.

Nationality: Many a politician has run into deep trouble with an offhand remark about particular nationalities. As a speaker, you'll have to stay on the right side of the fine line between condescension and caring involvement in any comments that refer to the heritage of a particular group. To be safe, you might want to enlist the assistance of a trusted member of the host organization.

CHAPTER 7

Ready, Aim, Persuade!

Perhaps the most valuable thing you can do once you've analyzed your audience is to target your efforts at persuasion. Decide which segments of your audience deserve primary attention. Dividing attitudes along the scale of one to ten (with one being hostile and ten being fully supportive), your most profitable area would probably be the fours, fives and sixes—the slightly opposed, neutral and slightly favorable segments.

A governing premise regarding the art of persuasion is that attitude change or behavior change is motivated by the audience's perception of a personal need or rationale for change—be it real or imagined, conscious or subconscious. This premise, the keystone of motivational psychology, sends a very strong message to you, the persuader: *Seek to establish linkages between your image and substance goals and your audience's needs.* Clarify and vitalize what your message holds in store for them.

Abraham Maslow, whose work in human psychology 30 years ago still remains as a model, said that there were five basic needs that motivate an individual. He ranked them from most fundamental to most advanced, and theorized that before one can progress from a lower to a higher need, a level of satisfaction has to have been met:*

---

*Abraham Maslow, *Motivation and Personality*, Harper and Row, New York, 1954.

> *Physiological needs:* The urges and needs required for survival, including eating, sleeping, shelter, sex and other bodily functions.
>
> *Safety and security needs:* Self-protection and security of families and societies (extended to patriotism).
>
> *Social needs:* The drive to form liaisons and join groups.
>
> *Esteem:* The desire or need for approval from others.
>
> *Self-actualization:* the feeling—often fleeting—of significant accomplishment and attainment of major goals.

The persuader, then, should analyze carefully how his main ideas or arguments can yield greater satisfaction of the audience's needs than the current circumstances or than a proposal favored by your opposition. Motivational speakers, a popular crop nowadays, play on the audience's needs for heightened self-esteem and self-actualization. Insurance men and firms that sell burglar and smoke alarms appeal to our physiological and safety and security needs. If you can't find something in your speech even remotely related to your audience's needs, then your speech requires major revision—if not the round file.

MAJOR MOTIVATIONAL STRATEGIES

There are several possible motivational strategies for persuasion, but three most commonly used are association, balance, and reinforcement.

1. Association: You've seen the ads where the man who uses a particular shaving cream soon finds himself surrounded by gorgeous women, or the woman who smokes a particular cigarette will be approached by the man of her dreams. A strong persuasive tactic is to seek to associate or link a position with an idea, ideal or individual highly regarded by the audience. Similarly, a way to discredit an argument is to associate it with a person or position disfavored by the listener.

2. Balance: It is difficult for most persons to maintain two contradictory beliefs—an imbalance of ideas. A speaker can attempt to upset an audience's equilibrium by pointing out inconsistencies between the audience's beliefs or between their beliefs and behavior. The next step, then, is to convince the listener that the speaker's alternative will restore the sense of balance.

3. Reinforcement: The easiest strategy to take when you and your audience agree on most things. Your role is to provide links from already-held beliefs (undisputed by your presentation) to logical extensions or expansions of those beliefs.

THE HOSTILE AUDIENCE

What strategies and tactics does a speaker employ when facing an audience that is openly hostile: a corporate president with unhappy shareholders or a dissatisfied union group; a political speaker taking an unpopular position, and so on?

Simply put, the main strategy must be (1) to be determined to be heard, and (2) to seek out areas of mutual agreement and common interest (association and reinforcement). Generating credibility is critical, for it helps overcome the tendency of listeners to transfer their hostility from the speaker's ideas to the speaker himself.

Seeking "common ground"—emphasizing areas of commonality and agreement between yourself and the audience—can be particularly helpful when there is a sharp division between you and the audience. But you have to be very careful that what you say sounds genuine and not forced. While it may be true, saying that "some of my best friends are black" will backfire every time. It sounds patronizing and forced; thus, the common ground is diminished, not enhanced.

An especially effective tactic when facing a hostile or skeptical audience is what I term "the preemptive strike." If you know the strong reservations the audience holds about you or your ideas, deal with them early, directly, and respectfully. For example, one of my clients who was seeking his party's endorsement for a seat on his state's Supreme Court had an impressive legal record, but no prior judicial experience. The lack of judicial experience was obviously a gnawing issue, and to combat it, early in his endorsement speech he mentioned two respected state Supreme Court justices with no prior judicial experience and three U.S. Supreme Court justices who fell into the same category (Justices White, Powell, and Rehnquist). My client won the endorsement by a 23 vote margin—133 to 110.

PLANNING AHEAD TO KEEP THE AUDIENCE'S
ATTENTION

To assume that an audience will listen to you hold forth for the duration of your speech because of your position in the corporation or due to the inherent interest value of your topic is at best naive. If any reasonably safe generalization can be made about audience members, it is that their attention spans are hardly impressive—constantly in need of nurturing. In fact, most research conducted on attention indicates that our normal attention span ranges between five and 20 seconds.

Surely, your credibility, dynamism and the inherent interest value of your subject matter should help maintain the plateaus of attention and minimize the valleys, but more is needed. And the responsibility is clearly yours. As one perceptive speaker once noted: "If you find anyone sleeping in my audience, come and wake *me* up."

I have already stressed the importance of linking your message to the audience's needs, one of the more significant means of capturing and maintaining attention. In addition, consider exploring the attention-getting potential of the following factors:

Familiarity: A major fire in your home town will normally interest you more than a fire four states away.

Curiosity: How long is the average person's attention span—less than a minute? A minute to two minutes? The curiosity (and surprise) generated by these questions heightens audience involvement—hence attention.

Humor: While I won't make a stab here at being humorous, think of how you can perk up when someone you like wants to tell a joke.

Conflict: To what extent do you watch a debate because of your desire to witness the verbal clash between the contestants? To what extent does the explanation of a conflict someone is experiencing in his job or family heighten your attentiveness?

The unusual or the novel: A client of mine who recently spoke about robotics decided to use a colored slide of a robot performing in a Detroit car assembly line. Since most had never seen an industrial robot, approximately 300 people were drawn to full attention.

CHAPTER **8**

Researching Your Topic and Checking Your Logic

In pulling your speech together, you should take time out for reflection. Outline what you *do* know. Think about the subject—the things you've seen, the people you've met, the places you've visited. Often the most compelling element of any presentation is "eyewitness" testimony. What can you offer?

As soon as you know you have a speaking engagement, do something to get ready for it. Write down on a piece of paper the ideas you think you might want to impart, or make a telephone call to ask somebody on your staff to start thinking about possible ideas or about conducting research. And make a step-by-step schedule for how you will tackle the assignment. *In short, do something productive to break the ice instead of leaving everything until the last minute.* Remember: *procrastination is the sire of speech anxiety.*

Search your files. A writer or a speaker should become a bit of a pack rat. Keep your notes and memos, magazine articles and newspaper clippings, committee reports and other memorabilia that might have any relation—no matter how remote—to an upcoming engagement.

After you've searched your own resources, talk to those on your staff and those you know in the field. Play reporter again, and interview them. Don't be ashamed to ask the most basic questions—tell them you want to hear *their* thoughts and *their* definitions to help you communicate your message.

Your next step may be your company library or a university or public library. There may be books on your subject, but they are likely not to be the most current material. For example, ask the reference librarian for assistance in researching the *Reader's Guide to Periodical Literature* for listings of magazine articles; *The New York Times Index* for daily newspaper stories in that publication; and the various specialized directories and indexes available.

If your presentation includes commentary on individuals, check *Current Biography, Who's Who in America* and similar resources. If the subject is of recent interest, read the index to *Vital Speeches* (a publication you should consult regularly anyway for its reprints of contemporary speeches by America's corporate and political leaders).

Your local newspaper almost certainly maintains a morgue of newspaper clippings and background material, and many publications will allow the public supervised access to the files. Many newspapers have indexes; some are published and available in libraries, such as *The New York Times Index*. Others are available only through the newspaper itself.

Your next step may be to contact one of the hundreds of specialized associations and groups around the country: the Edison Electric Institute; the National Cable Television Association; Common Cause; the Sierra Club; the American Association of Retired Persons; and the like. You may be a member of several of the groups. Or you can find out about them from the *Encyclopedia of Associations*. Since many of the groups are located in Washington, in New York City, or in state capitals, you may be able to find names and addresses in the Yellow Pages. Talk to the public relations or public information department of the organization; they may well have a press kit (or even a speech kit) available.

MINING WASHINGTON

According to a recent survey, more than 3,000 trade and professional associations maintain offices in Washington. Add to that lobbyists, special interest groups and foreign embassies.

Perhaps the greatest source of information and ideas, however, may be the federal government itself. Your Congressman's or U.S.

Senator's staff may be more than willing to assist you in tapping available research sources. You can go directly to a specific committee or subcommittee in Washington by finding the right name in the *Congressional Staff Directory* (P.O. Box 62, Mt. Vernon, VA. 22121). The executive branch is listed in the *Directory of Key Government Personnel* (Hill and Knowlton, 1425 K St., N.W., Washington, D.C. 20005).

Many of the Washington resources are brought together in one place in the *Washington Information Directory* (published by Congressional Quarterly, Inc., 1414 22nd St., N.W., Washington, DC 20037). This book lists by subject government committees and private organizations.

And there is the Library of Congress, probably the world's greatest single source of information. The press information office there can often direct you to a specialist within the agency, or to the library's computerized list of 12,000 organizations around the country.

If you need to determine the status of a specific piece of legislation, you may be able to gain the information from the staff of your area representative, or you can go directly to the telephone information services maintained by Congress. There are also several recorded message services, maintained by both the Democrats and the Republicans in the Senate and the House. These messages, updated hourly when Congress is in session, will announce the day's agenda and the results of any votes taken that day. You can obtain the current phone numbers through your representative in Washington.

THE ELECTRONIC RESEARCHER

And finally, there is the still-developing area of the electronic "data base." More and more bodies of information—from newspaper morgues and clippings files to statistical abstracts of census data to instantaneous coverage of world events and financial news—can be accessed through a computer.

The computer need not be an expensive, huge mainframe, either. And it doesn't have to be in your office. Most microcomputers and many word processing computers can be linked into one or more of the services. These devices include home computers and tiny portable computers no larger than an electric typewriter. You'll need only a terminal, a printer or a memory device, and a telephone line.

Companies that sell access to their data bases include the Dow Jones Company (with up-to-the-minute stock quotations included) and *The New York Times*. Dow Jones, as an example, offers access to a computerized file of *The Wall Street Journal, Barron's* and the *Dow Jones News Service*; transcripts of televised financial talk shows; an electronic encyclopedia, plus a full range of financial research tools including Securities and Exchange documents and stock price histories.

There is also a growing number of companies that specialize in a broad range of telecomputing services. The SOURCE, a subsidiary of *The Reader's Digest*, includes access to wire service news reports, economic and financial analyses, listings of Congressional schedules, direct access to Congressional research materials, travel and other services. CompuServe offers a similar range of services, plus specialized newsletters and listings of major stories from regional newspapers around the nation.

SUPPORT OR EVIDENCE

The research process will produce not only ideas, but support or evidence to clarify, vitalize and substantiate those ideas. The support can exist in the following major forms: examples; statistical or numerical information; expert interpretation; and real evidence (photographs, the gun found at the scene, a model of a nuclear power plant, etc.).

Deciding what support to use, how to use it and how much should be used is entirely a subjective series of judgment calls. Nonetheless, bear this principle in mind: *the priority areas of your speech requiring support are those most crucial to accomplishing your image and substance goals, including those ideas which are most controversial and therefore most prone to opposing argument.*

Whatever support you choose, make sure it passes the following tests with flying colors: relevant, recent, authoritative, potent, and sufficient.

- If the support isn't *relevant* (and check carefully, for first appearances can be deceiving), then the other tests need not be applied.

- *Recency* is a subjective criterion, rooted in the audience's perception that nothing major has developed since the evidence was gleaned to render it outdated.

- *Authoritativeness* should normally register the perception that the source, whether it is a person, institution, or publication, was able to make a careful, relatively unbiased judgment regarding the issue being discussed.

- *Potency* involves the inherent interest value and persuasiveness of the support; the language, tone, and length of the evidence can be as persuasive as—or even more persuasive than—its intrinsic merits.

- *Sufficiency* merely forces you to examine whether or not you have chosen enough support to clarify or reinforce your idea. Once again, more evidence should be considered if the idea is central to your image and substance goals or especially controversial.

Some caveats:

- When choosing examples to support your ideas, make sure they are more the rule than the exception.

- If the example is short and crisp, you might want to select one or two others to accompany it.

- When selecting statistics, be ready to defend the way they were determined as well as their relevance, remembering the famous line: "There are three types of lies—lies, damn lies and statistics."

- When selecting authorities, be prepared to state their credentials, remembering that prestigious institutional affiliations like Harvard or Princeton can be impressive to one audience and too highbrow for another.

CHECKING YOUR LOGIC

As you assemble your speech or case, you are formulating a conscious or subconscious pattern of logic which, in essence, becomes a skeleton for the progression of your ideas and their support. During this process, you must take care not to create short circuits in your reasoning process—or in your audience's. Some common examples:

Arguing in circles: "Capital punishment should be outlawed because it is inhumane; it is inhumane because it should be outlawed." There are many considerably more subtle variations of this sort of circular argument. It is an example of "closed" logic, an argument which falls apart under examination.

Argument to the person: A shift in focus from the issue to the person or group involved. For example, you probably will have to look no further than the most recent political election. "Senator Jones' third cousin was arrested last year on drunk driving charges. Where does Senator Jones now get the right to talk to us about the morality of nuclear disarmament?"

Unreasonable extrapolation: Although part of the process of logical proof requires generalization—moving from a specific example to a broader conclusion—an argument must not seek to make unreasonable extensions. An example might be in the realm of long-range economic planning. Economists may be able to predict events and conditions a few months down the road; although their assumptions may be logical, they have a dismal record in predicting trends for ten years from now.

The "non sequitur" and "post hoc, ergo propter hoc" arguments: Pardon the Latin! The "not in sequence," or the "after this, therefore because of this" arguments are positions in which a cause and effect cannot be demonstrated to be followed logically. As an example: "Productivity was down last week, which happened to be the week the percentage raise for the new year was announced. So apparently the employees are unhappy with the raise." The statement may or may not be true, but it is certainly not provable from the information given.

Argument to tradition: "My mother did it this way"; "This village has always done it this way"; "If it was good enough for us 50 years ago, it's good enough for us today." Or, "That is the way this company has always done business." There is no inherent logic in this sort of argument. However, overcoming the position can require arguing against sentiment—a near impossibility in too many instances.

Argument to authority: A close relative to the argument to tradition. It carries the implication that a certain position is valid because it has been accepted or recommended by the "experts" or by some outside authority.

Lifting out of context: The politician says, "We must maintain a strong national defense becase there is always a possibility that we may have war, and we should be prepared." The next speaker's fallacious summary begins (or an out-of-context newspaper headline might read), "We may have war, says...."

The suggestive question: Begging the question by presenting an assumption or assertion along the way. "Since your program obviously won't prevent street crime, what do you propose to do about protecting our elderly citizens?" Answering the question without challenging its assumptions puts you, at least at the start, in agreement with its position. (This type of question is discussed in detail in the chapter on question-and-answer sessions).

Argument by tone: Closely related is the sort of assumption or assertion by the internal tone of a question or statement, also called a "self-evident truth." "Obviously..." or "It is clearly evident..." should not go unchallenged unless the assertion is evident or obvious.

False alternatives: The assertion that everything is either black or white. "We must either raise taxes or cut spending." If there are other alternative solutions—and there frequently are—an either/or argument is not valid.

Mistaking chronology for causality: If a black cat crosses our path before we fall into the gutter, we make the assertion that the two events are related. In fact, they merely followed each other in time; any other assertion is unproven.

Confusing an effect with a cause: The ancient Egyptians supposedly believed the ibis had magical powers; shortly after the birds would arrive each year, the Nile would overflow its banks and irrigate the fields. The fact that the birds and the farmers were both dependent upon the Nile's cycle was apparently not considered.

Coincidental or concomitant variations: It is quite possible that a researcher will turn up the "fact" that in the period from 1970 to 1980 the number of persons on death row increased by 500 percent at the same time as the price of strawberries declined by half. The statistical correlation may be extremely high, but the relation between the events has to be established.

CHAPTER 9

Organize by Outlining

Before you say a word, you've got to prepare your message—regardless of whether you're going to read a manuscript or speak extemporaneously.

Any message receives a better hearing when it is presented in an organized and logical manner; in fact, a vivid, persuasive and well-supported message might well be lost if the listener cannot process easily the information you are presenting.

At the same time, the stronger your own sense of organization, the more confident you are likely to be in your overall presentation, and the more energized you may become in delivering it.

One of the best ways to prepare is to make an outline. Don't worry about following some rule book's description of the perfect form; whatever works for you is far better than nothing at all.

The structure you build should not be evident to the audience; you are constructing an internal skeleton, not a scaffolding.

Think in terms of a "subject sentence"—a central theme or thesis. Simplify the message as much as you can—let it be the foundation upon which you will construct a lofty and complex edifice.

Consider a pattern of organization. Some typically helpful patterns you might use are explained below:

Time pattern: An explanation which relies on a statement of chronology. Items are not necessarily presented in order of importance, but instead in the order in which they occurred

There were three major landmarks in the development of
the widget as we know it today.
A. First there was. . . .
B. Second. . . .

Topical pattern: The organization flows from divisions that are
obvious within the subject itself.

In order to examine the history of the widget it is necessary
to consider first function and then form.

Spatial pattern: Some subjects are best suited to an organization that is divided according to location or source.

An American widget is very different from a Chinese model.

A. In China . . .
B. In America . . . , etc.

Causal pattern: Best used when dealing with events.

The failure of a widget can have many causes.

A. Poor design
B. Poor quality control

Problem—cause—solution: Best used when advocating a policy
change (also see chapter on testimony).

Problem: The housing market is becoming more and more
depressed.
Cause: 1. High mortgage rates are making potential home
buyers wary.
2. A general lack of confidence that the economy will
improve feeds their wariness.
Solution: The Federal Reserve Board should enact policies
which result in more encouraging signs for mortgage-grant-
ing institutions.

In presenting a problem—cause—solution proposal, the speaker
must decide which area of his case is the center of controversy—
the problem?—the cause?—or the solution? If, for instance, most
of the audience agrees that a problem exists and essentially agrees
about its nature, then the speaker would be well-advised to focus
most of his persuasive energy on the causes and solutions.

Again, there is no one right or wrong organization for an outline. You might find it best to use combinations of techniques or
a special approach for an unusual topic.

SOME OUTLINING HINTS

Your outline should be your map—a visual representation of the road you will take in presenting your message. In its early stages, it should notify you if you have not adequately prepared yourself, and point the way to areas where research is needed.

Keep each line to one idea. The point is to allow the speech-writer, or the speaker who will use the outline for a direct presentation, to grasp quickly the point at each stage of the logical outline.

Check over your work to make sure that the order is indeed a logical one, with sub-topics subordinate to main points.

Some extemporaneous speakers will go through three separate drafts for an outline:

1. A complete sentence outline used in earliest stages of preparation.
2. A key word or key phrase outline used for rehearsal.
3. Speaker's notes in outline form for the presentation itself.

Here is a sample outline stated first in complete sentence form:

I. Select a specific purpose.
   A. Phrase your general topic.
   B. Consider your purpose.
   C. Consider limiting factors.
      1. Audience
      2. Occasion
      3. Alloted time
   D. Restate your topic to fit the limitations.

II. Develop a rough draft of your outline.
   A. List, in rough form, the main points you want to cover.
   B. Rearrange these main points in a logical sequence.
   C. Insert and arrange sub-points under each main point.
   D. Make a general note of the supporting material required for each main point.
   E. Check over your rough draft to see that it covers your subject and suits your purpose.

III. Recast the outline into final form.
   A. Rephrase main points to make them concise and vivid.
   B. Write out the sub-points as full sentences.
      1. Are they coordinated with your message?
      2. Are they subordinate to the main point?

    C. Fully develop supporting material.
      1. Are the details pertinent?
      2. Is the support adequate?
    D. Recheck the entire outline.
      1. Are you comfortable with the form?
      2. Have you covered the subject?
      3. Have you met your purpose?

Here is the third section of the same outline in a short-phrase form:

I. Recast for final form.
    A. Rephrase main points.
    B. Write out sub-points.
      1. Coordinated with message?
      2. Subordinate to main points?
    C. Develop support.
      1. Details pertinent?
      2. Support adequate?
    D. Recheck outline.
      1. Comfortable with form?
      2. Covered the subject?
      3. Met the purpose?

And finally, the same section prepared as speaker's notes:

I. Recast
    A. Main points
    B. Sub-points
      1. Coordinated?
      2. Subordinate?
    C. Support
      1. Pertinent?
      2. Adequate?
    D. Recheck
      1. Form?
      2. Subject?
      3. Purpose?

A few final tips: Apportion the time you devote to each idea to its importance in fulfilling your specific purpose. It is indeed easy to get carried away making a point that interests you but diverts the persuasive momentum you need. Also, when you have a series of arguments or a series of support for them with the flexibility to arrange them any way you wish, always begin and end each series strongly—with the arguments or evidence that can most likely generate your audience's interest and belief.

Finally, remember again, whatever is included in your outline—no matter how you prepare it—should be virtually indispensible to accomplishing your image and substance goals. *Beware of including an idea simply because you enjoy talking about it.*

THE INTRODUCTION

Unaccustomed as you are to making a speech, *don't say so!*

That's just one of many ways *not* to start a speech—guaranteed flops that put you into a hole before you've gotten out your climbing gear.

Here are some more ways to start out on the wrong foot:

- "This is the first time I've done this...."
- "I'm not very good at speechmaking, but...."
- "My wife tells me I'm the most boring man she's ever met...."

These statements may all be true—in which case you should finish reading this book before you accept a speaking engagement. But you should leave it to your audience to discover your abilities.

But don't go all the way over to dull, either. "My topic for today is ..." or "I've been asked to talk about...." They're inoffensive, all right, but uninspiring as well.

What you're looking for, then, is something to grab the audience's attention and prepare them for some intensive and intent listening.

Keep in mind the lessons of persuasion discussed earlier. Your introduction is often the logical place to address your audience's reservations about you or your topic. You must also work to establish your credibility as a speaker and your competence to discuss the subject at hand. Get to the problem early, if you can.

And remember, the audience's attention span can often be measured in seconds. One of your goals must be to keep your listeners awake through attention-getting devices. Phrase your words in ways that evoke vitality, curiosity, a sense of novelty or other "grabbers." Be graphic—choose words that "paint" pictures in the minds of your audience.

Your speech is to the annual gathering of the National Widget Manufacturers Society. Some possibilities:

An attention-grabbing rhetorical question (or series of questions) or statement: "What would you do with a solid-gold million-dollar widget?" Or, "Every one of you could own a solid-gold million-dollar widget within the next ten years."

An appropriate quote from a well-known person: "Benjamin Franklin once said, 'You can tell the quality of a man by the type of widget he uses.' "

A startling or interesting statistic, appropriate to your subject: "In the 45 minutes since this meeting began, American widget-makers have produced 1,356 jumbos and 56,341 midgets, with a combined potential of 1.2 million kilocuries."

A personal story or an anecdote of relevance and interest: "You all know my company's famous 'Tom Thumb' widget— at least I hope you all know them, since we spend an awful lot of money on advertising. Well, let me tell you the real story of how they came to to be invented."

Appropriate and related reference to a current event: "I'm sure you've all heard the news from Washington today...."

Unusual or unexpected biographical information: "I've been asked to speak to you today because of my position as chief executive officer of Amalgamated Industries, and I appreciate the honor. But did you know that I'm also a former widget designer, and before that a stockboy in a widget warehouse?" (Be careful not to sound too egotistical.)

The challenge to your audience: "Ladies and Gentlemen, we have no one to blame but ourselves for the sorry state of the widget industry! It is my hope, though, that we can come out of this meeting tonight with goals and understanding that will put us all back on the road to prosperity." A note of caution here: Be careful not to set an impossible assignment—your audience may recognize it as such and tune you out, or they may blame you for failure if the challenge is unmet.

HUMOR IN THE INTRODUCTION—OR ANYWHERE ELSE

Effective humor can be indescribably fulfilling to the speaker and the audience and can carry with it the capacity to project the speaker's good naturedness, cleverness and quick wittedness. But many speakers, recognizing the obvious merits of good humor, sometimes become so fixated about being humorous that they fail to appreciate and discover the other fruits of clear, persuasive and inspiring discourse.

Consider this advice:

1. If you are not by nature a good joke-teller in conversation, don't invest too much energy in trying to tell jokes while delivering a speech.
2. If you have a good sense of humor, but are not a terrific joke teller, one-liners may be your preferred suit.
3. The event itself—the audience, setting and occasion—can often generate better and more naturally delivered one-liners than a team of talented speechwriters.
4. If you have any doubt about the joke or line being funny, try it out on your reliable critics, making sure that the context in which you intend to present it is very clear. If any doubt exists after this pilot test, forget the joke.
5. Guard carefully against humor that may be transparently or subtly sexist, ethnic, risqué, or racist. While you may normally want your words to be memorable, such jokes can make your words too memorable.
6. Be careful not to use humor as a mask to disguise anxiety or lack of preparation. Indeed, too many speakers don't know the difference between thoughtful discourse and a nightclub routine.

THE VISIBLE SKELETON

Your introduction begun, your next task is to give the audience a reason to pay attention—a *need to know* or a *need to listen* to your message. Elements of this have been discussed earlier, although an example seems in order.

[From a speech regarding recent changes in Federal tax law:]
"Through the new tax law your company can claim a significant tax credit for research and development—one that can save you tens of thousands of tax dollars."

And then there comes the *preview*—a device that has advantages both for the audience and the speaker—a description of the framework of your remarks. By telling the audience a bit about the ideas you intend to discuss, you may pique their interest; moreover, you can enhance your credibility by demonstrating the depth of your preparation. A positive side-effect of this device is that it reminds the speaker of his planned outline. But when facing a hostile audience, be careful not to reveal or "overdisclose" your arguments too prematurely.

The outline is just the first element of construction that a speaker may choose. Two supportive devices are transitions and internal summaries.

Transitions: An example—"Now that we have seen the importance of a good introduction, let's examine the body of a speech."

Transitions are bridges that help the audience feel and comprehend the flow of ideas in a presentation—particularly important because the reader cannot go back to reread an earlier section. Some examples of these connective words and phrases:

- *Indicating time*—previously, formerly, at an earlier time, meanwhile, in the meantime, since then, after this, thereafter, now, now that.

- *Making evident*—thereby, therein, in this case, at such times, under these circumstances.

- *Returning to the purpose*—to continue, to return to, to resume, once more, at any rate, as I have said.

- *Making reference*—as for, concerning, as related to.

- *Citing*—for instance, for example, a case in point is....

- *Summarizing*—to sum up, as we have seen, up to this point.

- *Judging*—therefore, so, consequently, accordingly, thus, hence, for this reason....

Internal summaries: An example—"So far we have seen that historical references and personal anecdotes are good devices to use in an introduction. Now let us turn to...."

You should occasionally give the listener a break by summarizing your main points, restating your central theme, and reminding the listeners of their personal interest in what you have to say:

> We have seen that widgets have always been an indispensable part of industrialized society; we have learned how fluctuations in the price of chicken wire have affected the number of sheep killed by coyotes. Have you ever carried this one step further and thought about the relationship between the feeding habits of wild coyotes and our national defense?

Internal summaries are ordinarily advisable when the exposition has been technical or heavy. The summary you give is not only a way to clarify the direction you've already given, but is also a way to set the stage for points to come.

AND IN CONCLUSION . . .

You've seized the attention of the audience; you've shown them why it is in their interest to listen; and you've laid out a plan and followed it in a subtle but apparent manner, reinforcing your points as you've gone along. What is there left to do?

Often, you need to remind the audience of what they've just been told!

Give some thought to the design of your ending. We've all heard speeches by politicians that seem to build to a stirring climax time and again only to keep on going. At the very least, this becomes frustrating and distracting. So, too, is a speech that suddenly and abruptly screeches to a halt.

Your conclusion should come as no surprise to your audience—either in terms of when it comes, or in terms of its content. One device you should *not* use is to announce bluntly to the audience that you have just entered your conclusion; there are subtler and more effective ways of disengaging from your speech. You can imply the ending is near by a change in the tone of your voice, you can use a connective phrase, or you can just begin your conclusion or summary. Don't worry, the audience will catch on.

These five elements can enhance a conclusion:

1. A summary: If the speech has been a complex one, with several important ideas and themes, a summary may be needed. The recap can be in the order presented in the speech, or it can be in inverse order (on the assumption that what was heard first has faded from memory). Note: See the excellent summary used in the speech reprinted in the case study at the end of this book.

2. Referring to the introduction: A good device is to refer to an anecdote or quotation used in the opening of the speech. "And so, we've seen that Ben Franklin was quite correct when he said that you can judge a man by the quality of widget he uses...."

3. Personal reference: Tell what the point of your speech was for you, and how it affected you. If you've prepared your speech properly, the audience should feel it knows enough about you to care.

4. Looking to the future: As a result of the points demonstrated in the speech, the following predictions can be made. . . .

5. Appeals for belief or action: Most persuasive speeches, particularly those advocating policy changes, require a carefully phrased, superbly delivered appeal. Gauging the right amount of force or emotion it should contain is often difficult. Therefore, this is a good instance in which you should seek feedback from your more trusted advisors or communication consultant.

A TIME FOR EVERYTHING

And finally, there is the question of how much time to devote to the elements of your presentation. The basic answer: "Whatever works is acceptable." However, one rule of thumb says the introduction and conclusion together should take up no more than 20 percent of your presentation, with the conclusion itself taking about half as much time as the introduction. For a 20-minute speech, this pattern might see a two-and-a-half minute opening and a one-minute conclusion.

For a hostile audience, it might be advisable to devote more time to developing your introduction, particularly to cultivate credibility. For audiences not especially familiar with your subject, it might be more worthwhile spending extra time on the conclusion, to reinforce your major ideas.

CHAPTER 10

Modes of Delivery

Joseph Montoya made it all the way from the tiny town of Pena Blanca, New Mexico to the U.S. Senate, but apparently not on the basis of his speaking ability.

At the 1974 National Legislative Conference in Albuquerque, for example, Montoya was scheduled to give a major address. It had been a difficult day, and Montoya had not had a chance to review the speech written for him. As he climbed the steps to the podium, a member of his staff handed him the speech and a copy of the press release that accompanied it.

To the horror of his aides and to the unnoticed amusement of his audience, Montoya began to read the press release instead of the speech.

"For immediate release," he began. "Sen. Joseph M. Montoya, Democrat of New Mexico, last night told the National Legislative Conference at Albuquerque. . . ."

The senator, in fact, read the entire six-page release, including the final paragraph, which noted that he had been "repeatedly interrupted by applause."

We've all been victim of at least one of these persons:

1. The deadly reader, who plows on, oblivious to all around him, reading lifeless prose from a sheaf of papers he has carried to the podium.
2. The blank starer, who begins his presentation reasonably well as

he delivers a memorized speech, but suddenly loses his mental place, and with it all he has to say.
3. The rambler, who has neither a written speech nor any pre-defined thoughts.

You're presumably reading this book because you recognize that none of these speakers, or their equally confused and confusing cousins, is communicating anything but incompetence. How then should *you* prepare to deliver your message?

There are four basic modes of delivery for speeches: from memory, reading from written materials, impromptu presentation, and extemporaneous speech. Let's examine the advantages and disadvantages of each mode:

Memorization: At one time it was expected that a speaker would write out a speech, commit it to memory and then deliver it without notes.

- Advantage: Memorization allows the speaker to keep precisely to the message and the words chosen.

- Disadvantages: Unless you're an accomplished actor, the speech, as delivered, often sounds stilted and unnatural. The process of memorizing a lengthy presentation can be very time consuming. The speaker is deprived of the important element of interaction with the audience—adapting and changing remarks based on audience feedback. And finally, your entire presentation could be ruined by a failure of memory.

Reading: Probably the most difficult of all types of delivery to do well, probably suited only for the most formal of occasions—a summit meeting of world powers, perhaps.

- Advantages: As in memorization, reading from a manuscript allows the speaker to keep to a predetermined script. Risks of ambiguity can be controlled in advance. It also allows for control of time, assuming the speaker has practiced the presentation. Finally, the written script allows for advance release of the speech manuscript to the news media. (But is the release of the full manuscript necessary? Would a press release with generous excerpted quotes suffice—or even be better?)

- Disadvantages: Reading is not conducive to a natural speaking voice, bodily movement and eye contact. Very little real meaning and feeling is conveyed. And there is little convenient opportunity for on-the-spot adaptation to the audience.

Both of the following modes are closer to the form of communication you use most often in our business dealings. You usually have at least some command of the subject you're discussing and can organize a message and transmit it conversationally and naturally.

Impromptu: Speaking that is done without specific advance notice or preparation. Probably best suited for short, informal talks. You don't necessarily need to *think* fast, since your brain already runs well ahead of your mouth, but you should be able to *decide* fast. Which of the many things that pop into your mind are worth saying, and how best should they be phrased?

- Advantages: Remarks are spontaneous, conversational and natural, all desirable elements of communication. It is probably the most admired speaking ability. When an impromptu speech is good, it is very good; it generates credibility, persuasiveness and even memorability.

- Disadvantages: The order of elements is unplanned and often muddled. Assertions are generally unsupported by evidence, or the speaker is forced to rely on memory for support.

Extemporaneous: Here, the speaker has selected and organized his ideas in advance and may choose to rely upon a mental or written outline. A good example is a well-prepared presentation by a teacher; he or she knows the subject, knows what should be covered, yet does not rely on a word-for-word reading of a text.

- Advantages: The language and delivery are natural, and adaptable to the audience's reactions. The speaker can maintain eye contact and use natural gestures and movements.

- Disadvantages: Losing the ability to use precisely the words you want and the possibility of leaving out an element of your presentation. Control of time can also be limited.

AND THE WINNER IS . . . .

What is your best course of action? Quite possibly a little bit of each—a "hybrid" approach.

Extemporaneous speaking is probably the best mode for you to use in your business communication, if you have the time for preparation and rehearsal and the requisite self-confidence. But it may pay for you to combine elements of memorization, reading and impromptu speaking in a single presentation.

Here's how that might work:

> The body of your speech is researched and prepared in outline form to enable you to speak *extemporaneously.*
>
> You *memorize* the first few opening lines and a stirring conclusion to enable you to present them with full force and conviction.
>
> You may *read* short passages (as naturally as possible!) when it is necessary to quote someone precisely, to use specific numbers, or if you are concerned that you might be misquoted on a sensitive element of your presentation, or if you're simply uncomfortable presenting the idea extemporaneously.
>
> You allow for *impromptu* adaptation during your remarks based on audience feedback or in reaction to the comments of a previous speaker.

NOTES VS. NO NOTES

This is one of the more gnawing questions facing so many presenters. Unfortunately, there is no hard and fast answer to it. One thing, however, can be said for sure: in most instances the use of notes does not rate as a sin as so many speakers have been led to believe. Nevertheless, there are instances in which the speaker's total freedom from notes can pay significant dividends in the image department: it can project him as brighter and more articulate than would be the case if he had relied on notes.

The major issue regarding notes, however, should not be whether or not they are used, but, rather, *how* they are used. In short, overreliance on them is closer to sin than having them in the first place.

A caveat seems in order. If you are determined not to use notes because you feel they can lower your audience's estimation of you, consider two important questions: First, are the notes the problem or is the problem the way in which you use them? Second, if you were to avoid using notes, how likely is it that you might forget something important to the fulfilling of your image and substance goals?

LECTERN VS. NO LECTERN

Lecterns normally present both a physical and a psychological barrier between the speaker and the audience. And that barrier is accentuated by the speaker's inability to appear spontaneous and natural behind a piece of furniture that spells f-o-r-m-a-l-i-t-y.

For these reasons, I normally recommend that my clients avoid the use of a lectern. There are, however, five exceptions: first, when a microphone requires the speaker to remain at the lectern; second, when speaking from behind a dais; third, when a manuscript is necessary; fourth, when others on the program are using it and you don't want to upstage them; fifth, when the formality of the occasion truly dictates its use, for example, a sermon or the annual meeting of a large corporation.

When a lectern is preferred for one or more reasons, you should act as if it exists merely to hold your notes or manuscript; therefore, you should *converse* as if the lectern doesn't even exist.

Some speakers prefer to leave the lectern during portions of their remarks and then return to it for security or to consult their notes. This can be reasonably effective if the speaker's return visits are smooth and infrequent. However, this is more often the exception than the rule.

IF READ YOU MUST

You can make it easier on yourself, but not necessarily better for yourself, if you have to read some or all of a written manuscript.

Traditional advice over the years has called for manuscripts to be typed in all capital letters, or using one of several special small capitals and large capital letter typefaces like ORATOR.

Graphic arts experts, however, contend that all-capital printing is more difficult to read. A reader scanning a line of type recognizes words by their top silhouette. In theory, if you were to cover the lower half of a line of lowercase print, you should still be able to read the words as readily as if you were seeing the whole letters. But the top half of a line of all capitals is difficult if not impossible to decipher, since its top silhouette is often a straight line across.

YOU'LL HAVE TO DECIDE FOR YOURSELF WHETHER THIS PARAGRAPH, SET IN ALL CAPITALS, IS EASIER TO READ THAN

A PARAGRAPH LIKE THE THE ONE ABOVE WHICH IS SET IN
UPPER CASE AND LOWER CASE LETTERS. AGAIN, WHATEVER
WORKS FOR YOU IS JUST FINE.

By the way, did you spot the typo in the preceding paragraph?
If you didn't see the THE THE, your eye got lost in the maze of
capital letters.

ADVICE FOR TYPING AN OUTLINE OR A MANUSCRIPT

The style of manuscript or outline typing you adopt can have
an enormous impact on your delivery. The following advice should
be particularly helpful.

1. Every page should be numbered clearly at the top and bottom.
2. Don't break a sentence, paragraph or main idea between two
   pages.
3. Don't staple the pages together. Leave them in a sheaf so you
   can easily slide them silently after a page has been read.
4. Consider using a Scriptmaster,™* a specially designed container
   for your notes or manuscript.
5. Begin each sentence in the left-hand margin. If sentences are
   set in paragraph style, you will have to search for the end of
   one sentence and the beginning of the next, a major source of
   delivery and anxiety problems for the speaker.
6. Create a nice balance between long, medium and short sentences. This allows you to vary your speaking diet between chunks,
   bites and morsels.
7. Begin typing as close to the top of the page as possible. This
   allows you to establish smoother and stronger eye contact with
   your audience.
8. Don't type too far down the page; leave a 4–5 inch margin at
   the bottom so your eyes are not drawn to your navel as you
   read.
9. Annotate delivery advice in the margin: "Use right hand," "Point
   to screen," "Pick up pace," "Slow down."
10. When using a manuscript, place in the margins key words which
    could help reinforce both your sense of direction and movement
    through the speech.

---

*™A Scriptmaster can be ordered from Brewer-Cantelmo, Inc., 116 E-27th
St., New York, NY 10016

11. Finally, if, like many speakers, you have a tendency to overlook ideas contained in your notes, no matter how well laid out they may be, experiment with this simple technique which I developed for two of my clients. Lay out each major idea of your speech in a large rectangle bordered in a different color. Thus, as you treat each idea, your eyes cover just the materials included in the rectangle.

CHAPTER 11

Getting Your Act Together—Practicing and Presenting

How do you get to center stage? Practice!

You know everything you can about the setting and occasion; you've researched the audience; you've prepared a speech. Now comes time for rehearsal.

Your rehearsals should not begin until you are satisfied with your speech. This is another reason not to leave the completion of the speech until the last moment. If at all possible, give yourself at least a week to practice for a major engagement.

How much practice do you need? Only you can say, but one rule of thumb says you should rehearse until you feel confident enough to walk out on stage then and there. You should rehearse enough to be thoroughly comfortable with your message and its presentation, but not to the point where you have begun to memorize it.

You may find that three or four run-throughs will be sufficient; an inexperienced speaker or one with a complex and lengthy speech might need to run through it ten or more times.

An important suggestion: talk your ideas out until you feel comfortable with them *before* you make an audio tape recording. Then, after you are comfortable with the way you sound, go to a video recorder if available—and consider seeking the advice of a competent consultant.

Don't practice sitting behind your desk or floating in your bathtub—unless that is the setting you will use for the actual engagement. If possible, for major engagements go to the very room where your speech will be delivered. If you can't do that, try to arrange for a simulation. If you expect to use a podium, have one in the practice room. If you will use a microphone and amplifier for your presentation, include these devices in your practice sessions.

The videotape camera and recorder can be your greatest allies. Arrange for tapings of your practice sessions and sufficient time to review the recordings.

Don't practice in front of a mirror, at least at first; it may do more harm than good, making you overly conscious of your body and undermining the naturalness that should spring from the comfortable flow of your ideas.

When you're working from an outline, you should change the key words between sessions to aid your memory and to keep the presentation fresh and natural.

Try to replicate the lighting conditions of the speech site—particularly if your presentation is to be videotaped.

If you plan to use visual aids, have them available for the rehearsal as well, and practice your delivery in the dim light of the projector. Practice your script with the projectionist, if you will be using one. He should understand his cues and you should make certain the audiovisual effects truly enhance rather than clutter your presentation.

THE SPEAKER AS PHOTOGRAPHER

When relating to your outline during your practice sessions and during the speech itself, think of your eyes as the shutter of an expensive camera. Photograph with your eyes the key words or sentences contained on your outline; lift your eyes to your audience to deliver the idea with maximum impact, making sure you don't drop them until the idea has been fully presented; drop your eyes to photograph the next key word or line—and so on. As long as you don't overreact to the momentary silence associated with the photography process, and if you practice this technique religiously, you will discover a whole new dimension to your speaking skill. And, of course, the better laid out your notes for this purpose, the sooner and stronger this skill will develop.

Time your speech—each main idea in it. Now is the time to fit your message to the time allotted to you, not when you're in the middle of your presentation.

Once you are comfortable, present your speech before a select audience of honest critics.

MAKE SOME CHANGES

Listen to your trial audience and pay attention to what the video tapes show you. It really doesn't matter if *you* feel you are getting your points across—if your honest critics tell you otherwise, you should consider a different approach.

And then stop the changes. Your last rehearsal should be as close to the final presentation as you can make it; if there is something you feel you must change, then you have not had your final rehearsal. But be careful of making too many last-minute changes; a cluttered outline or manuscript can clutter the mind.

MOUNTING THE PLATFORM

A speech of ten thousand words begins with a single step— from the wings to center stage.

You have found out in advance of the presentation, of course, what the setting will be—whether you'll be seated on stage to await your introduction, whether you'll wait off stage, whether you'll be called from the audience. You have examined the path you must take—seen whether there are any cables on the floor or steps you must climb.

You've chosen your clothing with care—not just an outfit that will show well while you're standing and speaking, but clothing that fits you well while you're seated. (See Chapter 3.)

Don't fidget, adjust your clothing or riffle through your papers while waiting for your turn to speak; it communicates a lack of respect or interest, or both, in the current speaker. Spend the time fine-tuning your analysis of the audience or the occasion. Listen carefully to the speaker to see if there is any necessary adaptation you must make in your own presentation: is he or she covering some of the same ground you have staked out? What kind of reaction is coming from the audience? Is this situation providing you with an opportunity to display your wit? (Some of the funniest lines are spawned just as the speech is to begin.)

UP AND OVER

Walk to center stage purposefully but calmly and with a sense of command—and don't hurry. When you arrive, take a deep breath. Arrange your papers on the podium if you will use one. If you want your suit jacket buttoned, do so before you walk across the stage. Look around at the audience to establish contact and command— to signal to them that their attention is wanted. A firm, but friendly, "good morning," "good afternoon," or "good evening" can assist you significantly. This is part of the *critical ten seconds*, a period during which your *presence* as a speaker is established.

Everything should have been set up before you came to the stage, but if not, now is the time to adjust the lectern or check the microphone position. *Don't tap the microphone or blow into it.* Your first few words and the reaction from the audience should tell you if the amplification system is working. If you have any doubts, ask the audience.

It is important that you feel physically comfortable as you stand to deliver a speech; so, too, you should communicate through your stance an open and relaxed manner.

Your weight should be evenly distributed on both legs to avoid "pogo-ing" back and forth. On occasion, your hand can go into your pocket (if that is a natural gesture for you, and if you can easily and unobtrusively change your position to allow you to gesture). Your hands and arms should not dangle loosely at your sides— nor be on your hips, clenched across your chest, locked behind your back or draped heavily on the podium.

Wait for applause to end before you start. Acknowledge your introducer. Then, when all is ready, begin.

As you speak, you want each audience member to believe individually that you have prepared your remarks and come to the hall specifically to speak to him or her.

Again, you must maintain the aura of being in command. You should appear alert and aware of the audience, and intimately involved in the ideas you are presenting. All of the elements of presentation should be brought into play—nonverbal uses of your voice and gestures, forceful delivery of the oral language you have planned.

If the audience is sending you no message at all, they're possibly asleep. Ordinarily, the audience will "tell" you when you're right on target, or when you're losing them.

Watch the faces of your listeners. Are they straining to hear you? Are they following your presentation? Are they restless and studying their watches? Are their expressions hostile? Friendly? Bored?

It is also possible that distractions will emanate from the audience or from outside of your shared environment—a crying baby, a wailing siren, a tray of dishes crashing to the floor.

Don't compete! Wait for the situation to calm before continuing. The audience is generally on your side—share the moment with them.

A MOVING EXPERIENCE

Your gestures and movements should be communicative without being distracting. At one time, classical instruction in speech delivery included a set regimen of gestures and movements tied to certain specific ideas and phrases. The effect was like that of a ballet—and, as you know, not everyone can look graceful in such a rigidly choreographed dance. Instead, your gestures should arise naturally from delivery. The more you are in command of your ideas and willing to communicate, the more natural your gestures will be.

WIRED FOR SOUND

As noted earlier, the setup for electronic amplification should be part of your regular advance work.

If you plan to speak without a podium, you might consider wearing a lavalier or tie-clip microphone with a long cord to allow you freedom of movement. Be sure to practice walking, to avoid tripping on the wire. A wireless microphone, which requires a special receiver, is another possibility. The wireless systems have shrunk to the size of cigarette packages, and obviously afford you maximum freedom of movement.

A microphone on a stand or attached to a podium requires you to be nearby—about a foot in back of the podium with the microphone six inches below the level of your mouth. The placement is important both for capturing your words and to be certain that the view of your face is not blocked.

Don't handle a microphone mounted on a stand as you speak; it looks unprofessional, it can affect sound quality and it inhibits free gestures. However, walking around the stage with an unmounted microphone can communicate stage presence.

Maintain an even, natural tone of voice; leave it to the sound technician to adjust the amplification level.

If, following the speech, you can field questions without the lectern, consider leaving it; that is, if you don't need a microphone or if the microphone can be moved by you. The audience will feel closer to you—and you will feel closer to them.

"TO SIT OR NOT TO SIT"

This is one of the more frequent questions asked during my seminars: "Is it O.K. to sit on the edge of the table while speaking?" While the answer depends on many factors related to the audience and the occasion, I normally say that the speaker should ask himself why he wants to sit. To mask his own speech anxiety (since sitting is normally more comfortable than standing)? To create a more informal atmosphere? To establish greater intimacy with his audience? Certainly, there are better ways to alleviate speech anxiety than sitting; hence sitting is far more justifiable if it is tied in to communicating—to change the tone or intimacy level of the presentation. But to be effective, it must be timed and choreographed carefully and not overdone.

FIELDING QUESTIONS DURING THE ADDRESS ITSELF

Normally, a speaker should complete his address before fielding questions. Three major reasons: first, interruptions can impede his persuasive momentum; second, such questions are typically parochial and, as a result, neither the question nor the answer adds much to the audience's understanding; third, the speaker often has difficulty knowing how to cut off questioning and return to the body of his presentation, regaining stride.

There are, however, two particular circumstances in which allowing for questions during the presentation may be necessary: one, when a well-rooted norm has been established for this practice by an important body you are addressing, for example, a board of directors meeting; two, when your presentation is so long or technical that you might be well advised to break it into discrete 10-, 15- or 20-minute segments, each followed by a 5 to 10-minute question-and-answer period with a general question-and-answer period to follow your presentation.

YOU'RE FORGIVEN

You're going to make mistakes. You'll leave out an important fact, you'll misstate a critical premise, mispronounce a word or a name, you'll sneeze or cough, hesitate in search of an elusive word or phrase. If the audience will never know the difference, don't point out the mistake. If it is important that you communicate the idea, don't be afraid to go back and restate it without apology.

If you sneeze or cough, say "excuse me" and continue.

You will impress more audience members with a sense of poise than with a claim to perfection.

You're now ready and everyone else is. Before you say a word, think positively, focus on your image and substance goals and on your ideas, look the audience members straight in the eye and communicate in earnest to earn the strongest reception they could offer.

CHAPTER **12**

Question-and-Answer
Sessions

You've completed your speech. Everything you've said was carefully planned, outlined and presented, as it should be. Everything was under control.

But now, instead of walking back to your seat in relief, you are facing a sea of hands, waving urgently to gain your attention to ask you questions.

First of all, it should come as no surprise. If you have done proper advance work, you will have agreed to—or asked for—a question-and-answer period during your introduction. If you don't want to answer questions, your hosts should be aware of that.

Why would you *want* to be exposed to questions?

1. It is an opportunity to demonstrate your credibility and sense of openness.
2. If you handle the question properly, you may be able to defuse critics.
3. A question period is a second opportunity to make the main points of your speech. Research has shown that your last remarks are often most remembered.
4. It is an opportunity to clarify or expand on points of particular interest to your audience.
5. It is an excellent way to find out what is on the minds of your audience, and also how successfully you have communicated with them.

6. It greatly increases audience interest and participation in your presentation.
7. For many speakers, as noted earlier, it is more comfortable to engage in the give-and-take of a question period than to deliver prepared remarks. Some speakers, as a matter of fact, will prefer giving a very short opening statement and then turn immediately to an extended question-and-answer period.

What are the possible disadvantages?

1. You may be exposed to questions on subjects for which you are not prepared.
2. You may be giving the floor to an unfriendly adversary.
3. If you completely lose control, you could end up being an unhappy observer at what had been your own presentation.

The disadvantages, though, were listed as "possible." Your basic guiding principle must be to *maintain command and control* of the situation. Most of the suggestions contained in the chapter on dealing with interviews with reporters are applicable here, too.

Here are some suggestions on handling yourself in a question period:

Before you say a word, you should have in mind your basic message. See how you can fit your image and substance goals into your response to the question, even if the connection at first blush seems rather remote.

Try to anticipate any difficult questions. You have no guarantee that the questions will be directly related to your presentation, either. Is there a matter of controversy involving you or your company that might arise? Practice your answer—first for content, then for style.

Make certain the question is appropriate, and does not contain misinformation, misstatements, or incorrect assumptions. Don't be baited by offensive words or phrases from the questioner. If the statistics used are incorrect, say so. If you doubt the accuracy of a statement, politely request the questioner to identify his source. Any element left unchallenged may be assumed to be correct by the audience.

Listen very carefully to the question. And avoid interrupting the questioner unless you feel he's taking too much control of the floor.

Pause reflectively before answering especially challenging questions. Jumping in without testing the water with your toe—without thinking first—can be a chilly experience.

Be sure that the audience can hear the question. If necessary, repeat the question, carefully recasting it to remove any offensive language. Repeating a question is also a good device to earn you additional time to think. But don't repeat the question if almost everyone heard it or you will probably make your stall all too transparent.

Stay cool. Don't argue with a questioner. If he has a valid point, admit it. If he doesn't, consider stating your disagreement politely—demonstrating respect for another point of view. Or you may want to stress some shared basic agreement. For example, "While we seem to disagree about means, we *do* agree on goals." Follow that with a bridge back to one of your other points. The audience will appreciate your graciousness.

Be tactful. Don't tell or imply to a member of the audience that his question is dumb; don't tell him you already answered that question. You might instead wonder if your presentation was as clear and as comprehensive as you had hoped. And don't over-patronize the audience member with "that's an excellent question" (often more of a stall than a sincere compliment).

Be personable. In many situations it may be advisable to ask the questioner to mention his or her name and affiliation or home town. Referring to this person by name during your response can project you as more engaging and even soften his or her contentiousness.

Don't hesitate to ask for clarification or to ask an audience member a question. This can help you formulate your thoughts better, prevent potentially embarrassing misinterpretations, and demonstrate genuine interest in the audience member's point of view.

Be compassionate. The questioner may be more interested in cathartic relief than in your answer—no matter how good it may be. If the person is expressing a grievance about your company, the government, or the world in general, *be a therapist first, then an expert.* "I understand how you must feel." "I'm sorry you had to go through all that red tape."

Don't be afraid to say "I don't know." In fact, perhaps the worst thing you can do is to fabricate an answer. No one expects you to know everything; you'll stay out of trouble and maintain your credibility by saying "I don't know" (and explain nondefensively why), or "I'll find that out and get back to you." And keep that promise if made!

Treat each answer as a mini-speech. Fit your message to the question and then provide support and clarification.

Monitor your body language. Don't turn your back on a questioner, unless it is to break contact. Don't fidget with your notes, take a drink of water or blow your nose while a question is being asked. And be sure to maintain eye contact with your questioner, until you are ready to move on to someone else.

A TERRIBLE SILENCE

It won't happen often, but it is possible that you may ask for questions and receive none. Don't let it throw you; you may have covered the subject so well that you've left no question unanswered. More likely, no one in the audience has yet worked up the nerve to be the first questioner.

- Try interviewing yourself. "You know, the last time I gave a presentation like this, there was a really excellent question about...." And then answer your own question.

- Try to raise some questions. "There are some areas I didn't get into in my presentation that might be of particular interest to you...." Or, you might have picked up an interesting question when you arrived early at the session. Restate it and answer it yourself—and, if you use a bit of embellishment or editing in rephrasing the question, no one will be the wiser.

- Institute your own "survey" of the audience. Ask them some questions, get them involved and thereby break the ice for a two-way flow of communication.

- Many speakers make use of "planted" questions from a confederate or "shill" in the audience. If you choose this method, you may be doing so at great risk. People have a way of disclosing—consciously or unconsciously—when they are working from a script. Indeed, your credibility could be severely harmed if the audience catches on.

Finally, if no questions come, thank the audience and depart.

THE DIFFICULT QUESTION

Potentially crucial to the speaker's ability to perform well during the question-and-answer session is his ability to listen to a question, understand what it means, know what type of question it is, and remember its elements. He must also, of course, have been adequately briefed on the issues related to the question, and be able to answer it persuasively in a manner compatible with his image and substance goals. This is a difficult task, but the skills necessary to accomplish it can be cultivated.

Listening to a question, particularly in a heated session, is not as simple as it may seem. As the question is being asked, the speaker may, for instance, be thinking about how he could have improved on an earlier response; about points unrelated to the question that he wants to make during the next response opportunity; about how well he is doing so far; and so forth. Compounding the difficulty may be the phrasing of the question itself. The questioner may becloud it with too much background information, or may state as part of the question an assumption or argument with which the speaker disagrees or a fact that he finds inconvenient. This may cause the speaker to tune the questioner out or to refute him internally while losing focus on the question itself. And to make matters worse, a speaker may be loathe to ask for clarification, fearing that the rephrased question may be even more difficult to answer or that he may appear unintelligent to the audience.

Remembering the elements of the question can also be complicated, for the reason just stated. Although taking notes might help some speakers cope with this problem, they are often reluctant to do so. This is either because (1) they do not want to sacrifice eye contact with the audience; (2) they are fearful that such behavior might communicate lack of intelligence; (3) they are confident that they can remember the elements of the question; or (4) they may not want to "remember" all the elements because one or more might be difficult or awkward to answer—or actually unanswerable. The speaker who wants a portion of the question repeated faces two possible audience reactions: he may appear forgetful, possibly even unintelligent, or earnestly responsive. The latter reaction is more likely if the speaker's credibility is reasonably strong and if the question is lengthy, awkwardly phrased, or festooned with sub-questions.

"BANANA PEELS"

Crucial to the speaker's effectiveness is his ability to handle questions that pose danger because of their phrasing. These questions, called "banana peels" because of the speaker's potential to "slip" on them, fall into 11 categories. Listed below are examples of each and the major options a speaker has in responding to them. Realize, meanwhile, that different circumstances might call for a response option more desirable than the ones presented here and that one question could actually contain several banana peels.

Type	Example	Major Options
1. Hostile	"Isn't your time-of-day rate policy really a gimmick to fill your own coffers?"	1. Point out hostility. 2. Show cool, non-defensive disagreement, taking exception to terms chosen. 3. Project righteous indignation without losing composure.
2. Speculative	"What do you expect union membership to be in this state in four years?"	1. Label question as speculative. 2. Generally, don't predict with any attempt to be precise; stick with optimistic generalities (if, of course, they apply).
3. Hypothetical	"If interest rates drop to 12 or 13 percent within the next year, would you still support raising the state sales tax?"	1. Point out hypothetical nature of question. 2. Refuse to answer because of phrasing. 3. Answer directly.

Type	Example	Major Options
4. Picayune/over-specific	"What has been the percentage of growth of the Department of Transportation budget since 1978?"	1. Label question as overspecific. 2. If you don't know, say so. (Sometimes you may need to explain in a non-defensive manner why you don't know.)
5. Leading	"Why can't this state attract more industry with one of the best labor forces in the nation?"	
	This question carries three assumptions:	1. If you agree or disagree with any of these assumptions, let it be known.
	1. The state is not attracting new industry as it should. 2. The state has one of the best labor forces in the nation. 3. The labor force should attract more industry.	
6. Value	"Which is a better choice for energy conservation, carpools or public transportation?"	1. Apply your definition of "better" without drawing attention to this term. 2. Point out the value term, define it and then answer the question. 3. Ask questioner to define it and then respond.

Type	Example	Major Options
7. Question Begging	"Isn't the main reason why we have so little available energy related to the significant shortages of the types of energy we normally rely upon?"	1. Point out politely that the question in essence argues in a circle—it answers itself without probing further.
8. Multifaceted	"How many workers are unemployed in your company? How has this level changed over the past four years? How does your unemployment rate compare with that of similar industries? What do you plan to do about the unemployment problem?"	1. If each facet can be remembered and answering all won't cause harm (assuming there is ample time), then answer fully in the order you deem most advisable. 2. If you can cause harm by answering a remembered facet, it is probably best to "forget" it. 3. Feel free to ask for a facet to be repeated if you are reasonably certain you forgot a "safe" one. 4. You may want to refer humorously to the number of questions asked. 5. If the questions cannot be realistically answered within the time allotted, say so; e.g., "perhaps it takes only a minute to ask all those questions, but it will take a lot more than that to answer them."

Type	Example	Major Options
9. Vague, Unfocused	"What do you plan to do to make this a better company in which to work?"	1. Define the question the way you wish—consistent with your persuasive goals. 2. Ask the questioner to clarify his focus.
10. "Yes-No"	"Your campaign has been funded mainly by PAC contributions, yes or no?"	1. If "yes" or "no" is safe by itself, answer accordingly. 2. If risky, point out how the forced alternatives can interfere with a presentation of "the full truth." Then answer the question.
11. Nonquestion	"Unemployment is climbing; inflation is still spiraling; we are in a depression and ought to admit it."	1. Ask for a question, noting the nonquestion. 2. Respond to the nonquestion in whole or in part, by assuming whatever question you wish from it that could enhance your image and substance goals.

NONRESPONSIVE INSERTIONS

Since the relationship between speaker and audience involves largely a polite, implicit struggle over who controls the issues agenda of the event, the speaker must find openings within the question-and-answer session—*regardless of the questions*—to stress his image and substance goals. Waiting too long may result in a lost opportunity. John F. Kennedy, Jimmy Carter, and Ronald Reagan were encouraged to use and did use this tactic in their presidential debates.

The nonresponsive insertion can take on three forms: (1) it constitutes the entire response, regardless of the question; (2) it is presented at the beginning of the response opportunity, then followed by a more appropriate response to the question; or (3) it may follow the appropriate response.

HANDLING THE HOSTILE QUESTIONER

Sometimes it becomes necessary to handle not just the difficult question but also the questioner. Perhaps the most difficult type of questioner to deal with is the "floor monopolizer"—someone who will not relinquish control of the microphone, or will not sit down until after he's asked a question and you have answered.

Remember that the audience normally is mostly on your side. Appeal to the questioner's and the audience's sense of fair play. Tell the questioner, "Other people are anxious to ask questions too. If I get a chance, I'll get back to you." Then move your head and body in an obvious direction toward another hand.

And, for goodness sakes, don't ask, "Did that answer your question?" or indicate nonverbally any lack of confidence in your response.

Additionally, you might want to steal a quick glance at another part of the room as you answer the hostile questioner. You're looking to see what kind of reaction is coming from the audience (whose side are they on?) and also to locate another questioner. Again, as soon as you can, break contact and go elsewhere in the room.

Or, you might also toss it back to the audience and appeal to their sense of fair play by saying something like, "I understand how you may feel this way, but I'd appreciate it if you would let me finish. If you want to have an opportunity to speak later, and if these people here would like to listen to you, it's fine with me." A person who persists in interrupting you after that answer is not likely to win much support from the audience.

If someone seems intent upon making a lengthy speech, take the first chance you get to interrupt firmly but politely, and ask that he present a question. The audience understands the ground rules, and will usually support you.

Quit while you're ahead and preferably with a strong, positive response to the last question. Therefore, once a fair portion of the heat has subsided and the audience is at least basically favorably disposed toward you and, if at all possible, to your message, you should bid adieu.

Moreover, don't let the questions go on and on until they die a slow, painful death. Instead, cutting off the questions while there are still a few hands waving will leave the impression of a high-powered, successful performance. (It often is good practice to make an arrangement with the host to cut off the session at a particular time, or following an unobtrusive signal from you.) If the introducer doesn't take the initiative in ending the session, have your getaway planned. "I've got a plane to catch at 2 p.m.," you could tell your audience, "but I'd be glad to answer questions for the next ten minutes."

You're showing your interest in the audience and your accessibility, while still setting a time limit. Your reason needn't be as compelling as an airplane flight, either—merely establishing a cut-off time because of other commitments is perfectly acceptable. And, if the question period is going well, you could show generosity by extending your time. In fact, one senator I know arranges for his aide to give him a fairly early and obtrusive getaway signal which the senator ignores to accentuate his willingness to remain with the audience to answer their questions.

CHAPTER 13

Speech Anxiety

We've all seen the comedian's old reliable skit:

> The speaker crosses the stage on the wobbliest of knees, grabs onto the podium as if it were a life preserver and then throws a quick, glassy-eyed stare out at the audience. He screws up the courage to say something, but all that comes out at first is a high-pitched squeak. Finally underway, he is three sentences into an obviously memorized recitation of a moribund speech when suddenly his mind goes blank. His mouth moves noiselessly for a few moments and then he proceeds to riffle madly through a stack of papers until they slip from his hands and fly across the stage. And then....

Why do we laugh? Mostly out of a sense of shared panic. We've all felt that way, or feared it would happen to us if we were ever called upon to make a presentation.

The *Book of Lists* refers to a poll conducted in the United States in which 41% of those asked to name their greatest fear listed *fear of speaking in public* as number one. The percentages fell dramatically after that—all the way down to number seven—*death*.

Now think about the most accomplished, polished speaker you know of—perhaps a talk show host, an elected official, a learned professor or a preacher. Would it make you feel any better to know that he or she is also anxious before an important engagement?

Three points here:

1. Nervousness is perfectly normal and to be expected before a presentation. It arises from a sense of pride in yourself; if you don't care what you look like or sound like, you should have no fears.
2. That nervousness can and should be used as a tool to sharpen your thinking and your presentation.
3. There is a secret relief from speech anxiety—dedication, preparation and practice.

ANALYZING THE CAUSES

A principal cause of speech anxiety is fear of the unknown or the unfamiliar:

—You might not know the *people* who will be in attendance.
—You might be in a *place* where you've never been before.
—You might be speaking about a *subject* that is new to you.
—You might be speaking at the wrong *time*.
—You might be *reading* a speech you are not comfortable with, or one prepared by someone else, which you are expecting to deliver *without practice.*

The solutions should be self-evident:

—Find out everything you can about the audience and the group itself;
—Perform sufficient advance work to find out about the place where you will speak and the arrangements on stage;
—Make certain you are speaking on an appropriate topic for your background, and perform adequate research and preparation;
—If you feel you're not at your best in the afternoon, don't let someone else set your schedule; and,
—Practice, practice and practice. You should deliver your *own* speech—even if it has been written by someone else. You should have spent the time becoming familiar with the material, learning the outline and practicing the phrases.

BEFORE YOU TAKE THE STAGE

The process of controlling anxiety should begin before you take the stage. The following advice might be particularly helpful:

Don't put yourself through a hard time on the day of the speech. You should have done your preparation well in advance. Today is the day to relax and clear your mind.

Eat lightly before you speak. Stay away from drugs—and this includes alcohol for all of us and coffee for many. You may think you're doing much better, but you may only be fooling yourself.

Arrive early enough to alleviate tensions produced by traffic and to mingle with some of the crowd before you mount the platform. This will help make the audience seem more "real" to you, and you more "real" to the audience. It will also help you get your speaking voice and gestures into "tune."

Try to find an opportunity to perform moderate exercises to relax your neck, shoulder and back muscles.

Consider tossing a few splashes of cold water on your eyelids to make you feel refreshed.

Remember, you are the expert!

TAKING THE STAGE

Winston Churchill said that he used to calm his nerves before speaking by thinking of his audience sitting in their underwear—it somehow brought the high and mighty down to size.

That may or may not work for you; for some audiences the result might be a full-grown smirk on your face as you stand up to speak.

The first few moments are the worst for most people.

—Try taking a few deep, easy breaths before beginning.
—Don't dive into a speech as soon as you reach the podium. Give yourself a moment to catch your breath, arrange your papers, take a comfortable stance and look at the audience and let them see you.
—Make certain you know the opening lines of your address. Use the time to make yourself comfortable.
—Address your first few sentences to a friend or a few friendly faces in the audience. Feed on their empathy to get you over the initial nervousness.

In my own engagements, I like to open up by asking questions of the audience. It gives them a feeling of involvement at the very beginning. A sprinkling of humor also helps reduce the tensions—theirs and mine.

An example from a speaking tour I made a few years ago:

"How many of you watched the Reagan-Carter debate? How many of you remember watching the Kennedy-Nixon debates? And how many of you remember watching the Lincoln-Douglas debates?"

You might also consider using a visual aid early in the presentation, particularly one that foreshadows an important section. This should give you enough confidence to start on a roll. Moreover, the act of pointing to the visual should alleviate some physical tension.

Finally, since so many speakers perform more fluently, naturally and persuasively during the question-and-answer period than during the speech itself, I often advise them to think of their speeches as answers to hypothetical questions posed by members of the audience. This mindset normally helps control their nerves and, as a result, enhances their performance.

FEAR AS A STIMULANT

Some horseplayers make most of their decisions on handicapping by strolling out to the paddock before a race. They're looking for a horse that has a bright, alert look in its eyes; that gives off an aura of energy, but is not so nervous that he is using up all of that energy kicking at the groom or the jockey before the race has begun.

So, too, you should be prepared to harness your fractiousness before a major engagement. You're going to be nervous; you might as well use the energy to give your presentation life.

Convert your nervous energy into gestures, purposeful walking, vocal variety, facial expressions and enthusiasm, and let your nerves be your slave and not your master.

CONTINUING THE CONFIDENCE-BUILDING PROCESS

It is important that you take opportunities to make presentations before many different types of groups. Start with small organizations and informal gatherings. Move on to more formal settings. After a while, making a major speech before a large audience will only be a small step forward from what you've already accomplished.

Don't overestimate the demands of the audience—make your presentation long enough to cover the topic but not so long as to bore; make it personal and relevant and therefore interesting.

You don't need to be thrilling; being competent and caring will win you big points.

No doubt about it, the key to alleviating speech anxiety is mind over matter. Before you say a word, are you ready to take control?

CHAPTER **14**

Visual Aids—Sights to Behold

Pictures can be worth a thousand words—or more—in communicating your message to an audience. They can also interfere with communication or even send the wrong message.

Two basic principles should be considered here:

1. The visual aid should do the job better than words alone would, and
2. The presentation should be "you plus visuals," and not "visuals plus you."

A good visual aid can save you time by presenting quickly a concept or object that would take many minutes to describe. It can also demonstrate efficiently a complex subject—like the workings of a machine. And, it can pick up the audience's interest quickly, helping to enliven the pace of a presentation.

SELECTING THE TYPE OF VISUAL

Different situations call for different media: How large a room? What kind of lighting does it have and how controllable is it? How far away will the last row of seats be? Is electrical, projection and screen equipment available? What kinds of amplification facilities are used?

Here are some possibilities, with some comments on their major respective advantages and disadvantages:

Flip charts: Good for small, informal groups. Preparation of full-size visual aids is time-consuming. Difficult to transport.

Objects: Bringing an actual example of your subject to a presentation obviously adds great realism to your presentation—but can the object be seen? An oversized model of the subject may be more visible, but may be very expensive or time-consuming to produce and cumbersome to transport.

Handouts: Putting a piece of paper into your listeners' hands can add audience involvement and raise interest in your subject; more likely, it may prove distracting to them.

Chalkboards: Again, good for small informal groups. The chalkboard permits spontaneity, assuming the speaker is at ease as an "artist" or at least able to print neatly. It requires, though, the ability to speak and draw—without turning your back to the audience for too long or too often.

Overhead projector: Transparencies can be quickly prepared on many photocopying machines, allowing use of cartoons, newspaper clippings, drawings and other art. The projector itself is located in the front of the room and you will be able to operate it while facing your audience. The room can remain partially lit. You are able to write on the transparencies to add details during the presentation, and additional transparencies can be overlaid on the original. Be certain the lens is aimed properly and focused. Transparencies should be in frames and you should have an orderly way of storing those used and to-be-used.

Slide projector: The process of producing a 35-mm slide can be slower and more expensive than overhead projector transparencies. Projected images, though, are usually sharper. Slides can include photographs as well as charts and tables and can be synchronized to a sound track. An operator can run the projector, or the speaker can use a wireless or cable controller to the machine. New computer-assisted devices allow artists to produce slides using a television screen and a keyboard. Room-lighting conditions, however, must be taken into serious consideration when planning to use slides. Can the lights be dimmed so that the speaker is well illuminated while the slide is projected sharply? Or do the lights have to be turned on and off too often to facilitate a sharp image of the slide?

Audio tapes: Can be used to add interview or special sound effects to a presentation. Requires integration into room's sound system or separate sound amplification and speaker system.

Motion pictures: If the depiction of motion is essential to communication—as in the explanation of a manufacturing process—films are often used. Production costs and lead time are high. The room must be darkened, and a skilled operator is often needed.

Videotapes: Tape is replacing film in many uses because of advantages in cost, time and convenience. Tape needs no processing, and the editing function is quicker and easier than that of film. Special effects, including titles and animation, are also cheaper and quicker because of new electronic technology.

Among the various types of charts and graphs you might use are these:

Circle or "pie" charts, best suited to show proportions, as in dividing up a budget into slices of a pie;

Line graphs, which show trends or variations over a period of time;

Bar graphs, for showing comparisons, and

Pictorial graphs, which are specially adapted for use as visual aids. An example might be a bar chart of wheat production, showing yearly figures in terms of representative loaves of bread.

In selecting information to be rendered visually, ask yourself the following questions

1. Does the aid truly *clarify* or *reinforce* your persuasive goal(s)?
2. Or, is it being used more to remind you of the idea you must explain—as an unnecessary crutch?
3. Or, is it being used more because your reliance on slides is conditioning the audience to expect them—even if they are unnecessary?

Remember: *The stimulation of the visual aid should exceed the spoken word's capacity to communicate the same idea.*

Using unnecessary visual aids, particularly in excess, can significantly diminish your command of the situation and, as a consequence, both your credibility and persuasiveness. Again: the presentation should be characterized as "you plus visuals," not "visuals plus you."

DESIGNING VISUAL AIDS THAT CAN PRESENT INFORMATION DIGESTIBLY AND PERSUASIVELY

1. Choose the right amount of detail. Too much detail often appears in two major forms:
   a. sentences and clauses when keywords would suffice, or,
   b. columns of data when one or more columns could be eliminated or the "bottom line" could be explained with or without a visual aid.
2. Recognize when charts would be superior to lists or diagrams.
3. Avoid presenting too many concepts on one visual. Keep visuals reasonably simple.
4. Make sure the technical information depicted is central to your persuasive goal(s). Or was the aid chosen more because it was conveniently available than because it was the right vehicle for the audience?
5. Use the available space wisely. Often the presenter, in designing the visual, does not take into adequate consideration the amount of space needed between lines or columns, or the positioning of a line along the horizontal or vertical axis of the visual; e.g., should a line or column be raised or lowered or be moved more to the right or left?
6. Make sure that letters and numbers are legible from the back of the room.
7. Take advantage of colors. One of the strongest advantages visuals have over the spoken word is their inherent capacity to stimulate via color. Transparencies, which are normally dull, can indeed be more attractive than they are if colored sheets are used or, more desirably, if they are prepared professionally with the attributes of 35-mm slides.

RELATING SMOOTHLY TO VISUAL AIDS DURING THE PRESENTATION

An aid can be well selected and designed but lose its impact due to sloppy presentation. In fact, this unfortunately may be more the rule than the exception.

1. Position the screen and yourself so that you can see what is being projected and everyone in the room can see you and the screen as well. Also, it might be desirable for you to have a photocopied reduction of your slide on your notes.
2. Stand close enough so you can point to the screen if necessary.

   Notes: When using an overhead projector, you have the option of pointing to the projector or to the screen. This choice is normally determined by
   a. whether or not you would normally be standing near the projector,
   b. whether you would be more comfortable pointing to the screen than directly on the overhead.

   Pointing to the screen with a metal telescopic pointer can be more commanding, and more natural, than pointing on the machine. But be careful not to tap—and possibly damage—the screen.

   Have a place for the pointer when you're not using it. Otherwise, you might have a tendency to play with it.

3. Check your carousel tray before you speak, making sure all slides are
   a. present
   b. in proper sequence
   c. projected properly.

4. For major presentations, prepare a duplicate carousel tray complete with slides. (Don't forget spare bulbs for carousel or overhead projector.)
5. Before the slide appears, offer a verbal lead into it, e,g., "Let us now look at the growth of the money market industry over the past five years." Thus, the audience should not first hear the click of the machine, then see a confusing slide, then hear your explanation. Indeed, the verbal lead smooths out the slide presentation considerably.
6. Make absolutely sure that the slides complement rather than conflict with your narration. This is definitely the major problem associated with such presentations. Speakers often project slides, failing to explain them, even talking about something not clearly related to them.
7. Allow the audience sufficient time to digest the "meat" of the slide. Actually clock the amount of time each slide should be shown and place this information on your notes.

8. At certain points in your presentation you may want the audience to read the slide without your narration. A moment of silence on your part can be most welcome, especially since presenters often "overread" their slides.
9. Remove the slide as soon as you are no longer referring to it. Leaving it on the screen as you move on will only be a distraction.
10. If there is a fairly to very long space of time between one slide and the next, you should either
    a. turn the machine off,
    b. use a colored blank slide (usually blue) to soften the light projected onto the screen, or
    c. use a black slide to block the light.
11. You may want to place a few slides in reserve for the question-and-answer period. Indeed, having a slide at your fingertips to amplify a response can be most impressive. Append an index of your "on reserve" slides and photocopied reductions of them to your notes.
12. If you're planning to use a videotape cassette, have an extra copy of the tape in case of problems. Check the cabling to television sets or video projectors and whether the tape cassette is compatible with the player you will use. Also, determine if television sets have been adjusted for proper color and sound. Is the screen or monitor large enough to be seen by the audience?
13. Finally, consider the general electrical requirements: Is there sufficient electrical power in the room to support the devices you will use? Have you brought extra extension cords (with both two- and three-pronged ends) to allow placement of machines away from outlets? Have you brought extra fuses and lightbulbs? Do you have tape to secure wires to the floor so no one will trip?

If you've taken each piece of advice given here to heart and done everything possible to defy Murphy's Law ("If something can possibly go wrong it will"), then a power failure is about all you can expect to go wrong—and you shouldn't worry too much about that.

PART 3

The Media

CHAPTER **15**

Press Relations—Your Secretary Calls

Your secretary calls you on the intercom. "It's that reporter Jones from the *Bugle*, sir. He says it's urgent that he speak to you right now. Something about our plans for the Salina Street plant."

The *Bugle*—the local newspaper that ran a piece last week listing all the complaints of the union against management; the paper that regularly features on its "environment page" poorly researched and often just plain wrong articles about pollution by some "expert" or another; the paper whose business editor lately seems interested only in running speculative and damaging articles about your company's proposed merger with Consolidated Corp.

And Jones, this freshly minted cub reporter assigned to the business desk, who doesn't appear to know the difference between a debenture and a denture, has somehow found a pipeline deep into your company and has been receiving all sorts of confidential information. And now he apparently has something on your super-secret plans to close the Salina plant and shift production to Taiwan.

Why should you even bother to talk to him? And if you do, wouldn't it be better—and easier—to simply deny any and all rumors about Salina Street, even though they're mostly true?

Wait! Before you say a word, consider a few facts of business life.

The media need you, that is true. But you need the media—sometimes to an even greater extent.

We live in a tremendously disparate society. Your company may have grown to the point where you long ago gave up any hope of knowing the names and job titles of all but a few of your employees. Your factories and warehouses are spread out in five different cities and towns in three different states. And your executives, hourly workers, stockholders and customers live tens, hundreds or thousands of miles away from corporate headquarters.

And, in the dizzying pace of modern commerce, you find yourself needing more and more information more and more quickly. The money markets in New York, the commodity exchanges in Chicago, the gold fixing in London, industrial diamond mine production in Africa, the latest wellhead figures from the oil fields of Oklahoma have all become daily needed news.

Further, though you'll never tell him, Jones' piece about union grievances offered you a painless way to find out some of the concerns of your workers before you sit down at the bargaining table.

And so, you need the media to know what is going on in the world around you; your employees and your stockholders and the government officials and the regulators all look to the mass media for their information about the world and about you and your company.

And if you choose to "stonewall" the press, you will appear to be hiding, to be guilty of some unstated but obviously very serious crime.

Now, can you afford *not* to talk to Mr. Jones of the *Bugle?*

THE NATURE OF "BUSINESS NEWS"

The business pages of our newspapers and magazines and the business reports of radio and television have changed greatly in the past decade or so, reflecting the general shift in journalistic emphasis to "investigative reporting."

No longer are business stories confined to the "what"—a new plant, a new product, a new executive. There is much greater emphasis on the "why."

This does not mean that reporters are necessarily anti-business. In fact, there is increasing specialization among publications and the writers who work for them, with reporters taking undergraduate and graduate courses in business administration, economics, and labor-management relations.

But by the same token, don't believe that the reporter is there—from his or her point of view—to help you. The reporter is after a story and usually doesn't care if your stock will plummet or soar as a result.

And, the newspaper or television station is also a business, and is interested in its own sales or ratings; you or your company are merely a raw product for their industry.

The key, then, is to find the point of convergence of interests. The media needs you for its business; if you find you need the media, as you almost certainly will, then you must find a way to work together.

Now about that story on the Salina Street plant. It's correct, but the company wasn't planning to announce the closing until all of the contracts with Taiwan were made final. Disclosing it now might foul up the deal and would certainly complicate negotiations with the union on the new contract.

But denying the rumor to the reporter would probably not prevent publication of the story. And you'd look like a fool—or a liar—when the plans are officially announced in a few weeks.

The fact is, as you are often too painfully aware, that most reporters or publications get their information from many sources—not just from your official public relations department handouts.

One of your most loyal executives may have let the word slip in an offhand remark to a reporter. Perhaps she merely mentioned it to her husband who dropped the word at his bowling league to a buddy who then told his neighbor who just happened to be the newspaper's circulation manager.

Or, maybe the reporter just happened to notice some unusual activity—surveyors or appraisers at the plant site or an unusual influx of Oriental visitors (confirmed by the flight operations center of your local airport). Many a major story has surfaced through sheer coincidence. Reporters are paid to notice things.

And the fact is, much of your business operation is not secret anyway. A reporter can find out about your employment practices from state and federal equal opportunity agencies; about your safety records from OSHA and state labor departments; about some of your financial plans from state and federal commerce departments. If your company is publicly held, there are reams of documents on file with the Securities and Exchange Commission, most of them accessible to an industrious reporter. And, if you really are pursuing foreign investment opportunities, there may be additional information available through federally guaranteed import-export loan programs.

What should you do, then, to engender good relations with the media?

First of all, as in every other area covered in this book, you should take the time to think *before* there is a crisis. Do you have a competent, well-informed public relations staff? Are you—or is any other likely company spokesman—prepared for such a role? Do all the executives and managers understand your company's policy on responding to inquiries from the media? You do have a policy, don't you?

And most important—has your company established a good relationship with the media—a relationship based on trust? There are two sides to that equation: implicit in trust *by* the media is trust *of* the media. A paranoid feeling that the press is out to get you is usually due to a misunderstanding of their role.

A MEDIA RESPONSE MANUAL

Your large corporation has a Chairman of the Board, a Chief Executive Officer, an Executive Vice President, ten vice presidents and division heads including a Director of Public Affairs, plus 125 senior managers.

Who does the reporter for the *Bugle* happen to reach when he calls for comment on a report that three workers have been injured in an accident on the loading dock? A high school kid working as a summer temporary who grabbed the phone in the shipping department as he walked by.

"Terrible accident," he says. "Looks like that frayed cable on the crane that all the men have been complaining about for weeks finally snapped. Got to run. Bye."

It's not the reporter's fault for calling your company, nor is he wrong in printing the comment—true or false—from your employee—identified or not.

Step back for a second and ask yourself this question again:

Does your company have a well-thought-out policy for handling media inquiries? And, is that plan made known to every employee, from loading dock helper to chief executive?

Here's what one media response manual might look like:

At Amalgamated Industries, our good image as a business and as a corporate citizen is one of our most valuable and valued assets.

What we have to say to the people of Maple Grove can affect that image, and affect all of our jobs.

Therefore, it is critical that media inquiries be handled by a person with the *background* and *authority* to do so.

It will always be our policy to promote good relations with the media, and through it to the public.

It is Amalagamated's policy to

—Disclose as much newsworthy information as possible *without* violating employee, corporate or customer confidentiality;

—Respond as quickly as possible to all inquiries;

—And to present a truthful, consistent message to the media.

The *only* employees authorized to respond on behalf of Amalgamated are the members of the Executive Staff.

No other employee is authorized to give *any* information to a reporter without specific clearance from a member of the Executive Staff.

If you are *not* an authorized spokesperson and you receive a call from a reporter, you should:

—Politely decline to answer *any* questions;

—Explain to the reporter that you are not an authorized company spokesperson;

—Take down the name, organization and phone number of the reporter.

Immediately call the Public Information Office, at 4–7343, and relay this information about the call. The phone is monitored 24 hours a day, seven days a week.

If you *are* authorized to respond on behalf of the company, you should determine:

—The reporter's name and the organization he or she represents;

—The nature of the information requested;

—The nature of the reporter's assignment;

—And, the deadline.

Do you feel qualified to answer the reporter's questions? If not, explain that to the reporter and promise him a return call from an appropriate authorized spokesperson. Contact the Public Information Office immediately with the details.

If you feel you can answer the questions, don't be rushed. If you need to check some facts, or if you'd just like to take a few moments to compose your thoughts, arrange to call the reporter back in a few minutes. Keep your promise!

In any case, fill out a copy of the "Media Inquiry" form supplied to you with the memo and dispatch it immediately. —In fact, have it hand-carried to the Public Information Office so the staff there will be aware of the reporter's interest.

If you have a complaint about a reporter or a news story, *do not* make any contact yourself. Refer the complaint to the Public Information Office.

If you have *any* questions about company policy or how to respond to the media, please contact the Public Information Office.

This is, of course, just a small sample of what could be contained in one company's manual. You might want to have two versions—one that simply warns all non-authorized employees to refer all calls to your Public Relations Department, and a second, detailed manual for authorized spokespersons.

You also might want to involve your personnel office or training unit and have them include a discussion of media policy as a regular part of the hiring and evaluation procedures for your company.

HOW TO ESTABLISH GOOD RELATIONS WITH THE MEDIA

1. *Be of assistance.* Offer to help reporters in covering their beats by arranging informal tours of your plant, meetings with executives and background sessions on technical subjects. Provide the media with photos and visual aids for use in illustrating stories about your company.
2. *Employ a competent and responsive public relations department.* The unit should include persons with media experience, understanding of your community and full background on your company. A spokesperson is of no use to the company or to the media if he or she is not fully informed on policy and operations. The department should be on call at all times—either with staff in the office or by telephone. Security personnel should

be advised of the phone numbers of key personnel if an emergency occurs at an unusual hour.

3. *Respond quickly to all inquiries.* This comes part and parcel with the requirement that your public relations department understands the media. A response after deadline is no response at all.

4. *Have a media inquiry policy for your staff.* And if doesn't hurt to tell reporters of your policy. You should also provide direct phone numbers of those persons authorized to respond on behalf of the company.

5. *Establish ground rules.* Don't try to put something "off the record" after you've begun to respond. (More about this later in the discussion of interview techniques.) Don't answer questions and then ask that your name not be used.

6. *Meet with editors and editorial boards.* It enhances your position as a corporate citizen and your understanding of the local media.

HOW TO ESTABLISH POOR RELATIONS WITH THE MEDIA

1. *By dishonesty.* If you are not frank, fair and factual, you are no friend. And remember—*they* are the ones with the printing presses and the television and radio transmitters—not you.

2. *By being uncooperative.* A deadline is a brick wall for a daily newspaper or electronic medium. Failing to return a reporter's calls or responding with information after deadline is at best useless and at worst little different from the bright red flag of "no comment."

3. *By trying to be an editor.* You have no right, under ordinary circumstances, to review any copy prepared by a reporter. Don't try to influence an editor on how to handle a story. You'll probably end up earning the story more attention than it would have drawn otherwise. And unless you have specific evidence that a story was misrepresented, it doesn't pay to complain when your 90-minute interview gains only 15 seconds on the air. What's done is done; think about a particular medium's definition of news the next time you seek coverage and see if your efforts can be targeted more precisely.

4. *By playing favorites.* Giving a hot story to one reporter rarely helps. You might get good play in one newspaper or on one television show, but the other media may decide to ignore the

story on general principle. And, they may become very leery of future dealings.

5. *Seeking to "kill" a story.* It almost never works and almost always results in frayed feelings. And the attempted "kill" can become the lead of the story.

6. *Complaining about a particular reporter.* Most media organizations will react just the way you would to an attack on one of your corporate "stars." Whatever the truth of the matter, the public stance will almost certainly be a vigorous defense.

SHOULD YOU ANSWER AN UNFAVORABLE OR INCORRECT STORY?

The evening paper hits the streets with a front-page headline trumpeting, "THREE HURT IN AMALGAMATED ACCIDENT." The sub-head reads, "Worker Says Crane Cable Was Frayed."

Where did they get that information? You know that your public relations department had very quickly acted to release an official statement: that the accident was apparently caused "by the unexpected failure of a steel supporting rod which had been installed and inspected only last week by federal safety officials." Several of the reporters had asked about the huge crane on the other side of the loading bay area. Moreover, they had been told it was not in use when the accident occurred.

Fuming, you turn on your television for the evening news. You know that the reporter for "Action News" had visited the plant and been given the company statement. And the station had been planning to use just that explanation—at least until the news director saw the first edition of the *Bugle* just half an hour before air time. In the remaining few minutes the story was rewritten by a different reporter, based on the unconfirmed second-hand information in the newspaper story.

"Three Amalgamated workers were injured today," the newscaster solemnly pronounces. "Action News has learned that workers had complained about a frayed cable on the crane for several weeks. Company officials had no comment."

Wait! Before you say a word: how serious is the case?

There is very little to gain in pushing a complaint merely because you don't like the angle (newspapers call it the "peg") taken by the reporter. If the story makes you unhappy but does you no long-term damage, it would probably be better to try to deal with the problem (if it is indeed a problem) over time.

In this case, though, there are several serious aspects to the story:

1. Your legal department is sure to squawk about any unrefuted claim that Amalgamated was negligent in maintenance of a piece of equipment.
2. If you don't respond quickly to the story, erroneous claims in the story will come back to haunt you time and again in coming days and weeks. Every newspaper and most broadcast outlets maintain "morgues" of clippings which they rely on for background. Years from now you might see a story that refers to "a previous accident at Amalgamated in which a frayed cable snapped, injuring three workers."
3. Once again, make sure your media response policy is in place and that all of your employees are aware of its provisions.

HOW TO ANSWER AN UNFAVORABLE NEWSPAPER STORY

Don't question the newspaper's right to inquire into your affairs; there is no way to win that argument.

Don't complain about the reporter's technique in pursuing the story. Let the editor draw his own conclusions when he sees that the story is incorrect. Show some understanding of the pressures and difficulties of publishing a daily newspaper.

Don't threaten to pull your advertisements. By the perverse nature of the relationship between the advertising department and the newsroom of most papers, you could be almost guaranteeing front-page coverage for all your dirty linen for some time to come if you choose such a tactic.

Your only defense is reasoned, specific rebuttal. Don't just say that the story is wrong—prove how it is wrong. Encourage the newspaper to go to the scene if possible. Allow access to witnesses. And, if necessary, authorize release of police or insurance investigator's reports.

In the case of the loading dock accident, the story is likely to continue for several more days. The "correction" may appear as a story in later editions—if you really move fast—or in the next day's papers.

Don't be surprised if it takes a really close reading to recognize that the new story is really a correction of the first. The lead might say instead, "Investigators now say that the loading dock accident at Amalgamated Industries on Thursday was caused by the un-expected failure of a new supporting rod, and was not the result of company negligence as first reported." Not exactly the ideal apol-ogy, but a clearing of your company name—at least for the record.

There are other ways to seek a redress of grievances in a newspaper:

- Some newspapers run a regular column of corrections. (Un-fortunately, the corrections are rarely presented with as much boldness, or as close to the reader's eye, as the original error.)
- You can draft a letter to the editor. A few tips: respond quickly while the issue is still current. Study the letters printed in recent issues for an idea as to length, style and tone. Don't be ar-gumentative; although your letter is addressed to the editor, remember your audience is the newspaper's readers.
- Many newspapers and magazines have allowed "guest col-umnists" the use of a portion of the editorial page. *The New York Times*, for example, devotes a full page opposite its ed-itorial page (called the "Op-Ed" page) for such responses to the newspaper's opinions and those of other writers. *News-week* runs a regular column called "My Turn." Again, study some recent examples of pieces which have run on these pages for style, length and tone.

RESPONDING TO AN UNFAVORABLE TELEVISION OR RADIO STORY

Television and radio present different problems and solutions. Though a few programs include a "letters" or a "feedback" segment from time to time, generally your effort should be to find a way to get your response or correction into the extremely limited time available in the news show.

Again, if it is merely a question of disagreement over the tone of a story or its implications, you can bring the matter to the re-porter's or to the station's news director's attention and hope the situation will not be repeated.

If there is a serious error of fact, most stations will include a correction. If you act quickly enough, you might even be able to reach the news director during the broadcast and have a correction made while the show is still on the air.

You do have some small additional clout with broadcast outlets because they, unlike print media, operate under a revokable federal license.

Under Federal Communications Commission (FCC) law and regulation there are two avenues open to you: the community standards measurement and the "Fairness Doctrine."

All broadcast license holders are required to maintain a file of letters commenting on the quality of their service to the community. This file must be made available for inspection by the public and by the FCC and is supposed to be taken into consideration at license renewal time. Often the promise (don't make a threat) of a letter for this file is enough to gain the news director's attention.

The Fairness Doctrine does not apply to questions of accuracy as such; it is aimed at the broader question of the presentation of contrasting points of view on controversial issues. The Fairness Doctrine is the reason for the disclaimers you hear when a radio or television station broadcasts an editorial.

If you or your company are attacked by a broadcast editorial, you should contact the station immediately and ask for the opportunity to respond. Actually, FCC regulations require that you be notified of such an editorial within 24 hours after broadcast and that you be provided with a tape or transcript and be offered station facilities for a rebuttal.

If you are not the primary target of the editorial—if the opinion affects all widget makers and not just Amalgamated—respond quickly and forcefully. The station is given latitude to choose among those seeking equal time, so make your case a strong one.

IF ALL ELSE FAILS

If your polite but firm attempts for correction of broadcast or printed media news stories or editorials are to no avail, there are several further steps to consider.

Mobil Oil Co., unhappy about editorial opinion regarding "Big Oil," chose several years ago to run its own commercials or opinion on television and in newspaper advertisements. In fact, its ads became a regular fixture on the Op-Ed page of the *New York Times*. And to maximize their impact, Mobil bound and distributed collections of these printed ads as "public affairs" pieces.

There are also state and national industry groups which claim some oversight for news organizations. One such is the National News Council (based in New York), which invites companies or individuals to present their unresolved complaints to a board of review. The result has no force of law, but a vote of censure can carry some measure of moral suasion.

And finally, there is the option of legal action for slander or libel. Your legal department is sure to advise you that such cases can be extremely expensive, time-consuming, and difficult to prove. Even if the newspaper or broadcast medium in question has made a grievous error, it is necessary to prove that malicious intent was involved. Gross incompetence is not sufficient. Remember, both your company and the newspaper or station are likely to still be there when the dust settles, and your relations will be none too good.

A POWERFUL CASE HISTORY

In 1981, the Alabama Power Company decided it was not going to take it anymore and went very public with its protests of what it claimed was incorrect reporting, editorials and letters in the *Alabama Journal* in Montgomery.

In one of a series of large ads, the utility responded to an editorial:

"A LITTLE OFF THE MARK"
On September 3, the editorial page editor of the Alabama Journal gave his opinion concerning the salaries of Chrysler Corporation executives compared with those of Alabama Power Company.

To set the record straight, we have reprinted the editorial as it appeared. And in the margin, we've included some of the facts that the writer failed to include.

[The ad concluded:] In order for you to understand Alabama

Power, you need the facts—*all* of them—presented in a clear,
objective manner. What you don't need are prejudiced editorials.*

The campaign was obviously not aimed at winning friends at
the newspaper. But, Stephen E. Bradley, then vice president for
public information, said later:

> We don't even care so much if they (reporters) like us or
> not, although we have good relationships with most media
> representatives in our service area. We do, however, want them
> to respect us and to realize that if their stories contain errors
> or if they write slanted stories or editorials based on factual
> errors, we will respond, and respond loudly. The next news
> story is the important one. We want reporters to write their
> stories looking over their shoulders. We want them to hear our
> footsteps.

THE EDITORIAL BOARD

Every newspaper has an editorial staff. It may consist of one
person or of several persons who specialize in various areas such
as local government, federal government, state government, the
environment, energy, etc. Frequently, an editorial writer wears many
hats and is expected to have extensive knowledge in several diverse
areas.

Some metropolitan radio and TV stations also have editorial
staffs, but they are small compared to those on newspapers.

Editorial people are a totally different breed of cat. Virtually all
of them have served their time as reporters and have elected to
remove themselves from the hectic day-to-day activities of
a reporter to the more sedate world of the paper's "Think Tank."
But that does not mean they have rejected their roles as news-
persons. They are very much news people, but with a different
approach.

Editorial writers have the opportunity to research a subject
before writing about it. They read voraciously, and it is their obli-

---

*Stephen Bradley, "Defusing Media Adversaries," *Reddy News*, January/
February 1982, pp. 15–19. The point-by-point rebuttal appeared in Birmingham's
Alabama Journal on September 3, 1981.

gation to keep abreast of all major developments in many areas of general interest.

The Editorial Page editor may seek you out for an interview, or you may want to seek him out to acquaint him with your company's policies and goals. An editor may be willing to meet you for lunch, but don't expect him to visit you at your office. You visit him at his office.

Editorial writers are usually great talkers. Your meeting with them, unless you're dealing with a crisis situation, will most likely be very informal, chatty and lengthy. While they are not looking necessarily for "hard" news that will go into the next edition, they are newsmen. Don't ever forget that.

Basically, though, they are seeking understanding and in-depth knowledge that can be used to bring their editorials into sharper focus. They are not easily swayed by current fads and they seek to reduce popular emotions over issues to a minimum. Editorial pages continued to support President Nixon long after the front pages were calling for his head.

Trying to prepare for an Editorial Board meeting is like fishing without bait—a pretty hopeless effort. You can bone up on likely issues that might be raised, and you might want to bring with you some of your colleagues, but don't be surprised if they pop questions like how your company expects to meet the competition developing in Peru in the international market.

You may also be pleasantly surprised to find some of the editorial people know many of your friends and some of your competitors. They are not as flamboyant as many of their compatriots in the newsroom, but they are exceptionally knowledgeable in many fields.

Do not be misled by their usually easy manner and casual questioning. They want background information. They will sometimes even check a story that appears in their own newspaper for accuracy if they have doubts based upon their discussions with the subject of the news story if the story seems to conflict with what they have heard.

Honesty and candor remain your best attributes when dealing with members of the editorial board. They will appreciate it and it will greatly enhance your chances of getting a fair shake when your corporation is covered by them.

WHAT DOES BUSINESS THINK ABOUT THE MEDIA?

A poll of American business executives showed that most believed that the news media (except television news) accurately and fairly report and interpret business news.

The *Business Week*/Louis Harris Poll* showed that nearly three-quarters (73 percent) of 600 top executives from major corporations felt television news coverage was biased against business. Nearly the same percentage felt the specialized business magazines were pro-business. General circulation news magazines ended up somewhere in the middle, with about 25 percent of the executives calling them anti- and 25 percent pro-, and half seeing them as neutral. Newspapers were regarded by about 40 percent as prejudiced against business interests, by 45 percent as neutral, and by 15 percent as pro-business.

According to Harris, the poll showed a substantial shift away from acceptance of television news as unbiased or favorable, compared to a similar poll seven years earlier. *Business Week* reported that "the souring of business leaders' attitudes towards TV news coincides, of course, with TV's significantly increased coverage of business in recent years. As a result of public concern over the environment, the OPEC oil shock, inflation, and most recently, the recession, economic and financial news has become a television staple. 'TV is the power medium,' says Lous Harris. 'It's visible, and it's influential. But it has to deal with things too briefly. And whenever a company makes the evening news, it's usually because it's an unfavorable story.' "

Does this mean that you should abandon all efforts to deal with television? Of course not. It means that you should redouble your efforts to present your very best case to the media, doing so with an understanding of its requirements and nature and always with the self-assurance that comes from proper preparation.

Business Week, Oct. 18, 1982, page 26.

CHAPTER 16

Electronic Media—When Television Comes Calling

Television—the Great Unblinking Eye—presents a communicator with the opportunity to send a message directly to thousands or even to millions of persons over a medium that emphasizes intimacy and clarity.

Television news is our principal source of information about the world around us; in the past 10–15 years its impact has virtually eclipsed newspapers and magazines. In fact, today, 60–75 percent of Americans get their news from television on what one writer calls a "fast-food-like diet": lots of color and visual appeal, short bites of information and not much meat to the story.*

But what is television news? No one, not even the practitioners, can give you a hard and fast definition. Basically, "news" is operationally defined by the editor—or in the case of television, by the news director or the assignment editor.

In most instances, television news is an event or announcement that promises to be of interest to a large number of the viewers of a particular television station. If you are dealing with a television station that covers a medium-to-large population area, you are likely to find that that definition excludes far more events and announcements than it includes. And, of course, the converse also applies;

---

*Communication Briefings, April 1983.

relatively minor items—hardly newsworthy in a more populated area—can be arresting features in less populated areas.

While the local pages or business section of a newspaper have room for some of the most minor or highly specialized bits of "news," television stations are, of course, limited by time rather than by space. Moreover, in their headlong chase after "ratings," television stations are often guilty of limiting their coverage to the most sensational rather than to the most important.

Further, television news depends upon one more inherent trait of the medium, something often unrelated to substance: TV is in essence a visual medium. Reporters and editors have to find ways to tell their stories with pictures as well as with words. That is why the most common television news story is the spectacular fire or the multiple-car accident, rather than the thoughtful analysis of municipal finance trends.

The demand for pictures also turns every quest for a story into a minor expedition. While a newspaper reporter can cover a story with a ten-cent pencil and a fifty-cent notebook, the television reporter can go out on the road with tens of thousands of dollars worth of electronic cameras, video recorders, microphones, lights, a crew, and even a helicopter. And although technology has brought great advances, including the ability to transmit live from "on location" to the main studio, these capabilities often result in increasing reliance upon equipment.

Therefore, put yourself in the position of the corporation owning a television station: you have hundreds of thousands of dollars tied up in electronic devices, trucks to carry them about and equipment to broadcast their signal; you have dozens of employees, including a stable of high-priced "stars"; you have a sharply limited amount of time (22 or so minutes in a half-hour news, sports and weather broadcast), and you are competing with other stations on the basis of your ability to attract and hold viewers. Is it any wonder that most television stations feel they can't afford to waste time and effort on stories that don't help their business win and keep listeners? Television assignment editors are paid to dispatch crews to "sure things" only.

How do you get a reading as to what constitutes the news on your local station? Assign a public relations professional to watch it for a week with notebook in hand. Analyze the type of stories that make it through the sifting process to the air. What were the visual elements? What was the local appeal? How could you sell your message in a way that matches the interests and the techniques of the station you are aiming for?

One good way to gain television time is to find a way to "follow" an ongoing story. If, for example, the station is running a series of stories about the American auto industry and your company is ready to announce a new program which will subsidize workers' purchase of domestic cars, you have a perfect "peg" to offer to the station. Perhaps you'll even want to move up the announcement to coincide with the present coverage. Think in terms of a picture; an announcement at a car dealership or at an assembly line presents a much more attractive lure than a "talking head" shot of you behind a desk.

Your contact at the television station will ordinarily be someone with the job title of "assignment editor." Call early—7 a.m. is often the start of their day. Keep the conversation short and to the point; the assignment job is one of the most pressured positions at the station. Stress the "people" angle of your story, and suggest picture possibilities. Leave phone numbers where you or other contacts can be reached during the day, and leave open the possibility of alternate arrangements if today's story doesn't work into the schedule.

And keep trying.

THE MECHANICS OF TV

If you've got a scheduled television interview, your first notice of the approach of a TV crew may be the rumble of a van into the parking lot or the clatter of a hand truck in the hallway. But your planning for the crew's needs should have started long before.

Checklist for interviews

1. Allow time for the set-up of equipment and testing; plan on a minimum of 30 minutes.

2. Although modern videotape cameras, recorders and television lights are battery powered, you should nevertheless be able to offer adequate electrical service if needed. Have your building electrician check outlets for sufficient amperage.

3. Leave the physical arrangements to the camera crew. Let them pick the most favorable location in your office for light and

sound. They may want to open or close shades, lower or raise a picture on the wall, or even move some furniture. Don't try to play director—they know what they're doing. However, be certain to take a good, long look at the room when they have finished and before you start your interview. Make certain there's not suddenly an open copy of *Playboy* on the bookshelf over your shoulder, or a newspaper opened to an embarrassing headline or to a picture of a competitor's product sitting on your desk. Leave the technical aspects to the crew; keep the message design to yourself.

4. A technician will probably attach a microphone to you—usually a tiny "can" that will clip to your tie or jacket. He may want to string the cable from behind and out of sight, hiding the cord inside your jacket. The most professional arrangement, used only infrequently, might call for running the microphone cable up a pants leg or under a skirt. The technician will probably ask you for a "voice check." Speak normally, in the tone you will use for the interview, until you are asked to stop. Don't say anything you couldn't stand to hear on the air!

5. If there is a light in your eyes, or if something else makes you uncomfortable, tell the technician before the taping begins.

6. During the interview itself, look directly at the reporter. The cameraman may be moving around, the lights may be shifted, the reporter may be looking straight down at a notebook or a stopwatch. The technician or producer may be frantically flashing hand signals at the reporter. Ignore everything but the subject at hand. Keep your eyes focused on the spot where the reporter's head used to be.

7. After you've finished your interview, it is very likely you'll be asked to remain in your seat while the cameraman changes his position to shoot over your shoulder at the reporter. This is called a "cutaway" or a "reverse." The shot will be used in the editing process as a bridge between subjects. You may find yourself engaged in pleasant conversation about the weather while the shot is being made; again, remember not to say anything you wouldn't want in the story.

8. You might also find that the reporter will repeat one or two questions directly to the camera. Listen in if you can and be sure that the question he says afterward is close to the one you answered. Object politely but firmly if it is not. You'll have no chance to do

this after the reporter leaves, so at least try to maintain control while he is in your office.

9. And finally, remember the *three golden rules of microphones.* One, there is no such thing as a dead mike. Two, dead mikes don't exist. And three, remember the first two rules.

TUESDAY NIGHT LIVE!

A recent trend in television news coverage—part electronic advancement and part show business—is a move toward more and more "live" coverage. You may come across it in the form of an invitation to a live interview on the set of a news show during the news; or technology may make your office or home into an instant television studio.

Live broadcasts generally use new microwave or even satellite communications techniques. You need not be concerned with the details, but you'll find even more demand for set-up time. The technical crew may have to find a way to beam a signal from your office down to a mobile transmitter in a truck—either by a short-range microwave broadcaster or by cable—or there may be other special requirements.

Perhaps the most difficult assignment will be to respond warmly to a interviewer who is not in the room with you. You may be able to see your interviewer on a small television screen or you may have to play only to a camera. In such instances, aiming your words at the cameraman might make you more comfortable.

DELIVERING THE MESSAGE

Although you are talking to the reporter, you are really speaking to the vast audience that will watch the news. Try to visualize someone (preferably a specific person you like and respect) sitting before the television screen in the privacy of his or her home. And then think of yourself as a guest in the living room; you don't want to shout at someone, you want to speak in a moderate tone—conversationally. You're being transmitted right into the room with these people. Therefore, your phrasing and actions should be intimate and friendly.

Body movements—appropriate gestures and non-verbal emphases—are a near-requirement of a speech in a large hall. On television, though, caution is necessary. You are being examined under a microscope at both transmitting and receiving ends. Passion is much better communicated by means of your tone of voice or look of determination, than by a wave of the arm or a wallop to the podium. Natural, flowing hand motions are, however, fine.

Remember also that you will probably have only a few precious seconds. Keep your message simple and direct, and keep coming back to the theme. (Read Chapter 12 on Question-and-Answer Sessions.)

If you flub a line or if you deliver an unclear answer, don't hesitate to restate your answer more concisely, if possible. The reporter would much rather have a good quote than a confusing, disjointed one.

As in any other encounter with a reporter, stay away from the "no comment" clause at any cost. We've all seen the effect; no matter how valid the reasoning for not wanting to speak on a certain subject, the words "no comment" transmit an instant "guilty" verdict to the audience.

You are also going to be on physical display. Give some thought to your grooming and what it says about you.

Clothing: Wear conservative, comfortable clothing. Avoid patterns that might be distracting. Dress as you would for any important semi-formal social occasion. Wear the color that looks best on you. There is no prohibition against ordinary business shades of gray or blue.

Remember also that you may be seated for the interview. Does your outfit look good in that situation?

Be careful not to wear distracting jewelry. Large gold or crystal earrings or a pendant can catch the television lights and be very distracting.

Makeup: Society's expectations—and those of television technicians—have changed over the years and it is no longer mandatory to have all persons appearing on television covered with dense facial makeup. But if you have a shiny nose or forehead, deep shadows under the eyes, a heavy beard or deeply veined hands, a light touch of "pancake" makeup can improve your appearance. Only the larger stations employ makeup artists, so a bit of advance planning and practice may be necessary if you want to tend to this yourself.

Eyeglasses: As in your choice of clothing, your glasses should not be so large or so unusual as to distract from you and your message. If you are comfortable without glasses, leave them off— it will definitely improve your eye contact.

PREPARING YOUR MESSAGE FOR TELEVISION

Sometimes it pays to work backwards. Look again at your local evening television news show. Listen to the messages that make it to the broadcast: the good ones are short, simple and to the point.

Let's step inside the editing booth of a television newsroom for a moment. The reporter has just returned from an interview at a local factory. She was on the scene for nearly an hour, the crew ran through nearly 30 minutes of tape—and she has one minute and ten seconds to fill on the "Six O'Clock Report," which is only an hour away. Those numbers are not unusual; often the disparity runs even greater.

The vice president she interviewed went on and on about the marvels of the new product the company was introducing, but the reporter has decided to summarize all of that in her 15-second introduction to the story. Instead, she runs the tape at high speed— the voices sounding like chipmunks—until she hears the segment she had marked with a great big red exclamation point in her notes.

It was a silver-plated gift. While the producer was moving around in the background adjusting a curtain that had flopped open, she and the vice president had chatted amiably. The talk had moved to production techniques and the vice president had noted that the assembly line for the new product would be the first at Amalgamated to rely completely on robots. She had signalled with her eyes to the cameraman and he had nonchalantly turned on his recorder. "We won't have to add a single damned worker," the executive had said with some pride. "The machines won't join the union, either. And this is just the beginning," he had said with a broad wink.

The reporter had flashed her most gracious smile, too, and then had moved in for an unexpected kill. "How will this affect the tenor of your labor negotiations beginning next week?" she asked sweetly. "We ... we're not going to announce it until next month," he had sputtered. "Hey, this is all off the record." The reporter continued to press, and this time the cameraman openly filmed the executive's reaction. Now all he would say was "no comment." But she had everything on tape—from the wink to the dropping jaw. Great television!

Not exactly the best example of masterful use of the electronic medium by an executive, is it? But it does happen that way, and it illustrates two critical points: (1) the "dead mike" rule, and (2) the fact that your message—as defined by the reporter—will be plucked out of many minutes or even hours of conversation and edited down to "an electronic moment."

What should you do, then, to maximize the chances of getting your message across? First and foremost, you should know what you want to say—the image and substance goals you need to project. Second, deliver that message early and often in the course of an interview. And third, make your statement specific, short and quotable—so that no editor can play with it.

The companion to the rules for dealing with the electronic media is this: *State your conclusions—"the headline"—first.*

Which delivers the quotable quote?

Q. Is Amalgamated going to continue to grow here in Maple Grove?
A. Well, if we can find skilled workers, and if we can continue to enjoy living in a village that offers a nice place to live for our employees, executives and their families, and if the economy improves, then I guess Amalgamated will stay here. Yes, I think that's about it.

OR:

Q. Is Amalgamated going to continue to grow here in Maple Grove?
A. Yes. Amalgamated will grow and flourish in Maple Grove for as long as this fine village does the same. . . .

Practice stating your message in several different ways—as a flat-out statement, as a "therefore" conclusion, and in response to a question which seemingly has no relation to the subject. No one has asked you about Amalgamated's future in Maple Grove and that is an important message you'd like to send. Now you're asked:

Q. Aren't widgets an outmoded and useless product, and won't Amalgamated have to make major changes in order to stay in business?

A. Widgets have been the reason for the establishment and the tremendous growth of Amalgamated Industries, and Amalgamated will grow and flourish in Maple Grove for as long as this fine village does the same.

This sort of strategy is especially apt in live television or radio appearances, where you may have only a few minutes in total to get your message across. If you're asked about apples and you want to talk about oranges, keep coming back to oranges.

Television interviews, like all the other situations discussed in this book, demand advance preparation and practice. Have someone on your staff play the role of the reporter, asking questions easy and hard, germane and irrelevant, polite and rude. And consider retaining a communication consultant who will work cooperatively with the executive and the PR staff in formulating and addressing strategy, plus analyzing those aspects of the executive's performance requiring attention.

TELEVISION TALK SHOWS

Talk shows present some very different opportunities. For one thing, most are not chopped up and edited down into little bits.

The first thing you should do for a talk show appearance is to find out everything you can about the ground rules and setting. If it is a regularly scheduled talk show, make it a point to watch several editions in advance.

Study the format: how much time are you likely to have? How will you be introduced? Will there be other guests on the set while you're being interviewed? If so, who? Is there a studio audience, and if so, do they become involved in the show? Is there a telephone call-in segment?

Study the host: how well prepared is he or she? Is he hostile to some guests? Does he show any particular political or ideological bent? Does he seem to seek out controversy? Is he more a questioner than a talker, or vice versa? Which banana peels does he typically place in his guests' path?

Remember that many of the people who watch talk shows do so because they like or enjoy the host, not because you are the guest. Rarely, then, does it pay to attack the host or argue too strenuously over a point; he's already brought his cheering section with him. Also bear in mind that not every local television show host is a Phil Donahue or a Johnny Carson, although many try to pattern themselves after one of the stars. Just be yourself and leave the host to his or her role.

Find out how you will get on the set: will you take your place during a commercial break or will you be expected to walk to a seat while the camera is on? On many talk shows and interview programs you will be introduced while seated; the director or floor manager will ask you to "acknowledge" to a particular camera. What he's asking for is a humble nod of the head after the host has introduced you. (From that point on, look at the host and leave the camera work to the technicians!)

If you are going to be walking onto the set during the show, study the route you will be asked to take. Watch for camera stands and cables on the floor. You'll probably be summoned to a wing of the stage by a technician and held there until the proper moment. When you are signalled to go on, walk with authority but not hurriedly to your position.

A walk-on presents a few extra difficulties to the producer in terms of getting you a microphone. Find out in advance what the procedure will be. The simplest situation uses a "boom" microphone, dangling from an arm over your head and just out of camera range. Try to ignore its presence. Another situation might have a microphone sitting on a desktop—the "Tonight Show" set. Or, you may be handed a small clip microphone by the host when you arrive at your seat. Discuss with the technician in advance where and how you should attach it.

For some reason, the chairs used on many talk shows seem to be designed to show you off at your worst; they're either too low and overstuffed, uncomfortably harsh, or swivel so easily that you could be continuously shifting direction during the show without even realizing it. Pay attention to the message you will give with your posture. Sit forward on the chair to appear alert and interested, with your feet and arms in a comfortable position. In a seated position, you will probably look best with your legs crossed. Don't wear a vest because it tends to darken your image, to bunch up and to retain body heat because of the intense lighting of the television studio.

If you have the opportunity to select your seating, and the engagement is more of an opportunity than an obligation, try to sit next to the moderator; that's normally the power position.

You can be introduced two ways by the host: (1) If you are merely introduced by name and title without a "welcome to the show" directed at you, nod gently and pleasantly. (2) If the introduction and welcome are directed to you, say "thank you" (adding host's name) or feel free to choose another suitable amenity.

Refer to the moderator by name without overdoing it. Remember Dale Carnegie's saying (somewhat paraphrased) that the sweetest sound to any person's ears is the sound of his or her own name. Moreover, by being personable, you can impede the moderator's possible contentiousness.

Look at the moderator, unless one of the other guests is speaking. And again, don't try to upstage the host on his own show. Based on your analysis of the show and its moderator, work out in advance your expected lines of agreement and disagreement, and think of ways to fulfill your substance goals without sounding too contentious. Otherwise, you will surely jeopardize your image and your company's.

Act as if the camera is focused on you at all times. Although someone else may be speaking, the director may call for a shot of your reaction or may be showing a wide-angle shot of the whole set. Don't watch the red "on" lights on the cameras; you should be watching the host or the guest—whoever is speaking—with interest. Besides, if the show is being taped for later broadcast, it is possible that the pictures from more than one camera are being recorded for later mixing. Try to limit stretching, scratching, tie straightening, and other distracting body motions to commercial breaks.

As in all contacts with the media, you should have firmly in mind your basic message as well as your image and substance goals. Give short, easy-to-understand replies—without concentrating solely on reaction. Again, if the questions as phrased do not directly provide you with an opportunity to deliver your message, look for an opening. *Be proactive as well as reactive!*

Remember, although your tone and manner should be suitable for a conversation with an acquaintance in a small room, your message is actually aimed at the vast audience at the receiving end of the television signal.

If more than one representative of your company or group is on a panel with you, be sure to defer to that person or refer to his comments from time to time to communicate unity and, of course, to clarify your intended message.

And again, don't say anything during the commercial breaks or before or after the show that you couldn't stand to see broadcast or repeated.

Finally, have in mind a suitable amenity for the end of your appearance. Be prepared for a sign-off from the host which may be an effusive thank-you, or an earnest invitation to appear again on the show, or a quick, parting shot. A few suitable amenities:

"Thank you, Susan, for inviting me."

"It will be my pleasure" (to return to the show).

"I'll look forward to that, Susan" (to returning to the show).

READING A STATEMENT ON TELEVISION

There may come a time when you will be called upon to read, from a television studio, a statement replying to an editorial or making some major announcement or even preparing a paid advertisement for broadcast.

This situation is closer to delivering a speech. You may, however, have one advantage not ordinarily present in an auditorium—the use of a TelePrompTer or similar device.

The prompter projects an image of your written speech directly in front of the camera lens or just above or below. In one system, a special television monitor is mounted on the television camera itself. The screen points up at a see-through mirror glass in front of the lens; you see the words, and the camera lens behind the glass sees you. The effect is maintenance of eye contact with the camera and through it to the audience, despite the fact that you are reading your speech.

If the device is available to you, find out about system requirements before you arrive at the studio, and arrange for several practice sessions. You will want the operator of the prompter to move the words up the screen at the rate you normally speak.

The use of a prompter does not excuse you from practice and

preparation. Reading words off the prompter will still sound wooden if it's the first time you've seen them.

Try to visualize the audience as you speak to the camera. One device that may help you personalize your delivery is to have a friend or two stand next to the camera during your speech. If that is not possible, address your remarks to the camera operators.

But be careful not to become too reliant on using a prompter—a malady too many executives are developing; doing so may prevent you from becoming a natural television performer. Remember, the prompter won't be with you if an outside reporter is interviewing you with a minicam or if you're a guest on a local or national talk show. Key words, therefore, may in the long run be far more practical in many internal TV situations than full scripts.

DON'T OVERLOOK RADIO

People *talk about* television and newspapers, but they *listen to* radio.

Radio wakes us up, accompanies us to work in our cars, plays in the background in our offices and drives home with us. For millions of others, radio is a source of information and entertainment all through the day or night.

Radio's virtues include its immediacy; it is still the fastest with the news, no slower than the ability of a reporter to get to a telephone and call the newsroom. (Cable television's all-news stations promise to approach radio's speed, at least for the audio part of their reports.)

Another strong point for radio is its command of the listener's attention—greater than that for print or television media.

And uniquely, radio's phone-in talk shows can offer you both a good platform for your message and the ability to listen directly to the comments of your audience. Most cities have at least one call-in show, some radio stations are completely given over to the format, and there are several nationwide telephone shows on the air.

Radio gets much of its appeal from this openness and from its relatively expansive time constraints. Radio talk shows surely worked for the executive of a major brewery in Pennsylvania. The brewery was turned down by its union on a proposed contract the company said was essential to its survival. The president of the company made the rounds of the local radio talk shows on Friday and Saturday and discussed the situation with callers, many of them his own employees. In a second vote on Sunday, the contract was approved.

Appearing on a radio show gets you around many of the obstacles presented by television. You are likely to have more time to present your case; you are able to bring with you notes, documents and even aides. There is not the awful electronic eye of the television camera staring you down. You can take off your tie or your shoes and relax.

Many radio shows, in fact, don't even require you to travel to the studio. You can be interviewed and answer listeners' questions over your own telephone in your office or at home. The price of this arrangement, though, may come in the tone the host takes toward you; face-to-face conversations are often more genial and less forced than telephone calls.

Radio is much more compact in its equipment needs than television, and studios are considerably less formal. A typical studio is a small room dominated by a control board with tape players and turntables. At larger stations, the board and the various devices are operated by an engineer on the other side of a glass wall, with just you and your interviewer at a desk. At most stations, though, your host will serve as engineer, telephone operator and interviewer. He or she will seem to pay very little attention to you from time to time, attending instead to technical needs. But don't let your attention wander; you may suddenly be on air.

As with television talk shows, the host's questioning can range from brilliant to banal and from benevolent to brutal. I have appeared on a dozen or so radio talk shows within the past two years, and I can state with feeling—impressive moderators are a rare commodity.

Before you appear on the show, remember to define your image and substance goals and, of course, do your best to anticipate questions. One show I appeared on recently sent me a list of "possible questions" two weeks in advance (a most unusual circumstance). On another, the host showed me her list of questions before we went on the air, to which I reacted approvingly while unobtrusively noting the "banana peels" (trick and tough questions). Normally, however, the host doesn't know the question until it is ready to come out of his mouth—and sometimes does not even know it then.

Your general goal in appearing on the show may be to promote a book you've recently published or your services. Yet the host might not mention the book, the name of your firm or its location. Radio, unlike television, allows you to slip him a friendly note asking that this information be conveyed, especially if you might appear to be unduly self-serving in conveying this information yourself.

Telephone call-in shows usually employ a system that delays the whole show by several seconds to allow the cutoff of an obscene word or inappropriate comment from a caller. The delay should be of no concern to you; you won't even know of its existence unless the host dives across the control board to hit the cancel button.

In any radio situation, remember that the only way you have of communicating is through your voice. It is, as always, critical that you keep in mind your primary message. But you must also deliver that message in a way that is aurally attractive and clear. Think of the situation as a telephone conversation with a friend.

If you find yourself being harassed by a caller, you may find the host coming to your rescue. If not, treat the situation as you would a rough question-and-answer session and maintain your cool. (See Chapter 12.) Remember, the audience is most likely to be on your side when you're dealing with a hostile character.

Similarly, if you find yourself facing a hostile host (you should have known about him in advance through your preparations), don't try to out-argue him. It's most likely a battle where if you win, you lose.

Don't, however, be intimidated by the host either. Feel free to use the "banana peels" approach described in Chapter 12. Also, be on the lookout for "cliff hangers," potentially damaging statements the moderator slips in before the breaks for commercials or the news. If you feel the statement is potentially damaging, refute it at the first opportunity—but be careful not to sound too defensive or you may be inviting an unwelcomed debate.

THE MEDIA TOUR

Should you or one of your colleagues represent your company or your organization on a media tour? Or should you hire a well-respected celebrity who can be credibly identified with your service or product?

Surely, this PR tool has gained tremendous popularity recently—and why not? In the final analysis it is a potentially powerful yet inexpensive form of communication—that is, if effectively planned and executed.*

If the media tour is a tempting proposition to you, what basic qualities should the spokesperson have?

1. A sound understanding of the product or service.
2. A personable, confident manner.
3. The ability to be facile in the give-and-take of questions.
4. The ability to discuss the service or product without sounding too commercial.

A short case example seems appropriate. A few years ago the prominent New York public relations firm of Harshe-Rotman & Druck hired for their client, the Aerosol Packaging Council, Dr. Joyce Brothers. Her role: to help consumers overcome guilt feelings associated with their use of aerosol products in the home. And, as expected, her credibility helped carry effectively her main substantive message: that most of the aerosol products had been reformulated to eliminate the controversial fluorocarbons.

Once the spokesperson is selected and trained, key media markets must be chosen. In most instances, priority is given to major population centers which, due to the overflow demand for exposure on their channels and stations, are the toughest to schedule.

After the key markets have been targeted, the person in charge of the tour must develop a list of media contacts to approach in each city, including a list of shows most appropriate for promoting the product or service. Nine major reference works can greatly facilitate this process: *Broadcasting/Cablecasting Yearbook* (Broadcasting Publications, Washington, D.C.); *Radio Contacts* and *Television Contacts* (Larami Publications, New York City); *National Radio Publicity Directory* (Peter Glenn Publications, New York City); *Ayer Directory of Publications* (N. W. Ayer, Philadelphia); *Bacon's Publicity Checker* (Bacon Publishing Co., Chicago); *TV Publicity Outlets Nationwide, Cable TV Publicity Outlets Nationwide* and *New York Publicity Outlets* (Public Relations Plus, Washington Depot, Ct.).

---

*Many of the ideas presented in this section are based on "Managing the Media Tour" by Jeffrey Close, in *Marketing Communications*, January, 1981.

Generating the station's, newspaper's or magazine's interest in granting the interview requires two major tools of the trade: First, a comprehensive, well-prepared media kit with relevant descriptions, biographical materials and photographs. Second, polite persistence by the person in charge of the tour—both in writing (via a "sell" letter to the editor, program director or producer) and on the phone.

Jeff Close, formerly of Harshe-Rotman & Druck and now with Cigna Corporation, offers seven additional tips for making the media tour successful:

1. Be prepared. Know the subject, the market and, most of all, the media and their audiences.
2. Plan ahead and plan carefully. Remember Murphy's Law: "Anything that can go wrong, will."
3. Look for additional media outlets in each market. Often, a relevant trade publication will be based in a tour city.
4. Keep in touch with the spokesperson and the media. Interviews do get canceled, and knowing about cancellations early enough may permit the scheduling of a substitute interview.
5. Follow up. Contact editors and broadcasters to thank them for interviewing the spokesperson and to purchase tapes of the broadcast interviews and copies of the print interviews when they appear.
6. Be persistent. Don't wait for the media to initiate contact. Remember, the competition is fierce for space and time. Don't be annoying, though.
7. Make sure the spokesperson is prepared, well-rehearsed in communicating the message and *enthusiastic*.

If you now have even the slightest notion that the media tour may be for you, your company or your organization, consult with your major public relations advisor. You may be able to take advantage of a platinum opportunity.

"FRONTING"

One of the more popular and ostensibly effective advertising tactics to surface over the past five or so years is for the CEO to sell his company's product or service through television and radio commercials and printed advertisements. I call this tactic "fronting."

Lee Iacocca is the premier "fronter," having brought the Chrysler Corporation, within only five years, from the brink of bankruptcy into the black. Other CEO's who have shared at least a fair percentage of the remaining limelight—and with apparent effectiveness—are Avis' David Mahoney, Eastern Air Lines' Frank Borman, Remington Shaver's Victor Kiam, and, of course, the ubiquitous Frank Perdue of chicken fame.

When "fronting" campaigns are successful, their results are largely due to the credibility the CEO is able to project to the public. And that credibility is based mainly on the "safeness" and "competence" he communicates. Iacocca, for instance, projected himself as a strong, no-nonsense, sincere spokesperson who instilled confidence in the consumer—confidence that he had the requisite leadership qualities to keep Chrysler afloat and to stand behind his product.

While "fronting" may, at first blush, appear to be an imaginative tactic, it is actually a return to history. Less than a century ago most businesses were identifiable by the shopkeeper as well as by his product. Our grandparents and great grandparents could always rely on a specific person—a face—if their stove, furniture, or cloth goods proved defective. Today, in sharp contrast, corporations have become faceless giants. "Fronting," therefore, gives these giants a face—someone specific to identify with in addition to the product or the name brand.

If you are thinking about "fronting" for your company or organization, consider the following questions:

1. Do you project the image traits required for the campaign? (Note: Seek the most candid feedback you can.)
2. Can you perform—or learn to perform—superbly before the camera and under the lights?
3. Are you totally comfortable with the overall design of the campaign?
4. Are you prepared to accept the glory as well as the inconveniences associated with "star" status?
5. Do you have a persuasive response to accusations that you are seeking the limelight for personal gain or launching a veiled political campaign?
6. Are you aware of, and ready to accept, the consequences if the campaign doesn't work?

Tough questions for most CEO's. But Iacocca's success is good reason to pause and reflect—*very carefully.*

CHAPTER 17

Press Techniques—The News Conference

The news conference is the quickest way to get your message to the largest audience.

When do you call one? When you've got significant news to announce. A "no-news" news conference can easily backfire. Reporters look for stories, and if there are none readily apparent at your news conference, they'll fish for one. If a reporter returns to the newsroom with no story at all, his editor will be reluctant to assign a reporter to any future conferences you might schedule.

A small note: These events used to be called "press" conferences. It may or may not make a difference to you or to the reporters, but a television or radio station has no press.

The best place to hold a news conference may be in your own offices, especially if you have a room or auditorium large enough to accommodate the reporters and the television equipment. Will the presence of reporters or crews be too disruptive to normal business activities?

Other considerations include the following three factors:

1. *Acoustics.* Will reporters be able to hear you? Will you need a microphone? An amplifying system can present complications for broadcast reporters because of problems caused by feedback.

2. *Lighting.* Do you have your own television lighting (and does it meet the current specifications of TV cameras)? If not,

do you have sufficient electrical power and outlets to use port-able lights?

3. *Physical arrangements.* Do you have a table of sufficient size to hold a roundtable news conference? Do you have an attractive rectangular table for a sit-down conference? Do you have a photogenic lectern or podium? Is your company logo available for use as a prop or backdrop? Are there easels or other devices to support graphics and displays?

The news conference site should be made available at least an hour before the scheduled starting time to allow crews to set up cameras and microphones. The room should be stocked with rolls of "gaffer's tape" (wide cloth tape) for use in attaching equipment. The lectern should be placed against the proper backdrop—your logo or a neutral-color wall. Don't put the speaker in front of an undraped window; the light will blind the camera. Make sure there are no inappropriate pieces of art or wall hangings within camera range.

Picking the right date for a news conference is part careful planning and part crapshooting.

First of all, you should be reasonable. Select a date that will allow you sufficient time to prepare information and a message for the conference—and sufficient time to notify the media and to produce whatever materials are necessary for a news packet to be distributed to reporters.

Next, select a date on which there is no scheduled major news event that will conflict with your conference and, as a result, draw reporters, newspaper space and broadcast time from your confer-ence. If you are fortunate enough to select a "slow" news day, the "play" of your conference should be significantly better.

If you plan to rent a hotel room for the conference, you should check with the hotel management to see if there are any other events scheduled for the same day. Friendly assignment editors or reporters might provide the same assistance.

But if a plane crashes or a building burns or some other major news event happens on the day of the conference, you're going to have to be prepared to chalk it up to the breaks of the game. If there is enough time, you might consider rescheduling the con-ference; but be sure to notify quickly every reporter and organization you invited.

There are a few bits of information you can gather to help select the proper day. Work backwards from the immutable elements of your announcement. If you are committed to announcing a new contract on October 1, you have no choice as to date. If, however, you don't have such a strict deadline, think next about where you'd like to get your biggest play.

If the newspaper is your number one target, and if the paper has a large Sunday edition, you might want to schedule your conference for a Saturday morning. Saturday is also a very slow day for broadcast outlets—but bear in mind that most operations field only a skeleton staff on weekends. Other typically slow days are Mondays and the days immediately before and after holidays. There is nothing wrong with consulting friends among reporters for suggestions on the best day for a conference.

The next question is the time of day. Select your prime target and aim to meet its requirements:

Morning newspaper. The paper on your doorstep or your desktop in the morning was written between about noon and midnight of the day before. An early afternoon news conference will meet its needs as well as those of the nightly television shows.

Afternoon newspaper. "PM" papers are produced on a split schedule. Reporters typically work from dawn until mid-afternoon. Depending upon the size of the paper, its circulation area and the number of editions published each day, the first deadline for copy may be as early as 9 a.m. Final deadline— for the papers delivered to commuter stations—may be as late as noon or 1 p.m. Feature stories and analytical coverage are usually done during the afternoon, after deadline.

Television stations. Crews and reporters typically report about mid-morning and work into the evening. The best time for television coverage for the 6 p.m. nightly news is usually between about 11 a.m. and 2 p.m.

Radio stations. Radio is generally the fastest medium available. News can make it on air in the time it takes a reporter to get from your conference to a telephone. The prime time for radio news, though, is the early morning and late afternoon—called "drive time" in metropolitan areas.

PREPARING FOR THE CONFERENCE

You'll probably want to draft some *brief* opening remarks. Very few reporters will use the remarks in their stories; your purpose should be to paint a broad picture which sets the foundation for the fulfilling of your image and substance goals, to preempt with precise phrases any highly expected negative questioning, and to suggest areas for questions. The opening statement should also help to calm your nerves.

Working with your public relations director or other executives, draw up a list of possible questions. Don't limit them to the announced subject of the news conference. There is no rule that reporters must stay on the topic; in fact, it is quite possible that several may want to take advantage of your presence to pursue other stories. For that reason, try to keep abreast of all current news events, whether directly related to your business or not. There is no predicting how a reporter may try to tie your announcement or your company to some national trend or event.

Schedule practice sessions—in the news conference room if possible. Your communication consultant and associates should fire the toughest questions they can come up with. Get used to the room and its set-up. Turn on the television lights if you've got them. Make and then analyze your own videotape of the practice session.

Don't "scoop" yourself by allowing the details of your announcement to get to the media in advance. Caution your staff against leaks from within the company. It is quite possible that a reporter may call and try to wheedle a story out of you. Resist—and don't go "off the record." It's not in your best interest.

THE DAY OF THE CONFERENCE

Everything is ready. You have been fully briefed. Your public relations person has gone on ahead to the conference room to make sure everything is in place and to offer assistance to any early arriving reporters.

Give yourself a few quiet moments alone. Calm yourself, attend to your personal appearance, and go over your image and substance goals. Then proceed to the conference room a few minutes ahead of starting time. Shake hands with a few of the reporters—it helps make you more human in their eyes, and vice versa. You're ready now to head for the lectern.

Relax. Deliver your prepared remarks clearly, and use the time to get over the butterflies. (See Chapter 13.)

Now to the reason you are there: ask for questions. *Take charge and keep it!* You can try to set the ground rules at this time—you can say that you'd like to stay away from a particular subject and you can ask that the reporters identify themselves. Be prepared, though, for none of your requests to be honored. And, in some instances, setting a particular subject off-limits is roughly equivalent to waving a bold red flag in the eyes of a bull. Be certain you have a reasonable—and quotable—explanation for your demurral ("in litigation" being the most common).

Respond to questions in short, declarative sentences when possible. Don't forget to put forth your message early and firmly.

If you don't know the answer to a question and none of your colleagues can help, inform the reporter that you will get the information to him as soon as possible. Don't be afraid to admit there's something you don't know. It's a lot better than being proven wrong.

Remain cool. Remember that your purpose is to communicate *through* the reporters at the news conference to their much larger audiences.

Don't show impatience if you're asked a "dumb" question, or a question you've already answered. It is very important that reporters understand you. It is also possible that a reporter may have arrived late. And finally, a radio or television reporter may want to record you answering "his" question, and not the very similar one just asked by the reporter from the competing station. Or, the television crew simply missed one of your answers; they rarely leave their cameras and recorders running through a whole session.

Don't say, "As I already said before . . ." or offer any variation on this theme. It is condescending, serves no purpose, and it may ruin the value of your quote.

Similarly, you will probably be approached by one or more reporters after the conference for quick questions. There are two reasons for these "private" news conferences. Radio and television stations may want to make a tape—an on-scene report called an "actuality" in the trade—that showcases you and their "star." A print reporter may approach you with a question because he feels he has an "exclusive" angle which he doesn't want to share with the other reporters in an open conference. Or, perhaps his paper is on the other "cycle"; for example, if the morning paper will have the first crack at the story, the reporter for the afternoon paper will be searching for a different angle.

If you know a reporter by name, or if the reporter identifies himself, use the name in your answer. It helps to personalize your relations with him. This is particularly appropriate when you are dealing with television reporters; they are very much regarded as "personalities" by their employers, and are likely to include in their report any comments that show them interacting directly with you.

AN ELECTRONIC NEWS CONFERENCE

When Johnson & Johnson announced its plans to reintroduce Tylenol capsules in 1982, following the tragic series of poisonings which seriously damaged the product's acceptance in the American marketplace, the company decided to seek both national and local press coverage.

Chairman James E. Burke conducted a news conference from New York which was sent by satellite to 30 American cities, as he answered questions from reporters anywhere in the system.* This approach worked remarkably well; newspapers and television stations had their choice of a national wire service or network feed or a story by their own reporter, with any appropriate local angle.

Besides gaining entrance to a number of major markets at the same time, a tele-press conference also gains entry into smaller communities that might otherwise be bypassed or covered in a very expensive and time-consuming manner.

As with any news conference, the question of timing must be considered. And the message must be one that generates interest in greatly varying areas. An example: in 1982 two major automobile manufacturers announced their new models and made available their top executives to newspapers, radio and television stations.

If you take this route, you should provide full details on the technical arrangements for the conference to radio and television stations, including information on how they will be able to plug their equipment into the incoming video and audio signal to make their own recording. Some television stations may be able to receive the signals over their own satellite reception dishes. In other in-

---

*Several companies specialize in providing such multi-city hookups.

stances, reporters would have to go to a motel, a company facility, or a special teleconference site in their area.

There has to be some scheduling arrangement made for questioning—perhaps a pre-announced order for all participants.

Advance planning should also include distribution of press packets and other materials to the tele-news conference site.

CHAPTER **18**

Crisis Communication— Plan Ahead

A crisis, by definition, is something that breaks the rules of normal operations. But that does not mean that you cannot and should not plan ahead.

You have fire drills and you have disaster plans; do you have a crisis communications plan?

Here are some basic elements of a plan:

Your company's top officials, including but not limited to those designated as "spokespersons," should meet and get to know area elected officials, law enforcement and public safety officials. They should be made familiar with your company, and you should become familiar with their procedures for emergency situations.

Your spokespersons should know their counterparts at area hospitals, law enforcement and public safety agencies.

All of your employees should be made aware of the exist- ence of an emergency plan, and the company's media re- sponse manual should insist that any comments to representatives of the media *must* come from authorized spokespersons only.

DRAWING UP A CRISIS PLAN

Your first step should be the drawing up of a nightmare list. What could possibly go wrong? A fire? An explosion? The death of the CEO? Building collapse, riot, food poisoning, chemical spill, electrocution, hurricane, blizzard, crash, collision, epidemic? Don't rely solely on your imagination; talk to others, including engineers and maintenance people.

Next, develop plans that include techniques and procedures applicable to all potential situations. Add to it some specific procedures related to unusual occurrences; which events require an evacuation of your facility, which events require keeping workers inside?

Spell out precisely—by name, title, location, office phone, home phone, emergency contact means—the sequence of notification to be followed when an emergency occurs. Make it clear who starts the ball rolling. Make certain that the public relations director and other spokespersons are at or near the top of the list.

Make whatever changes are needed in advance. Your study may show that while your company has sufficient telephone service spread around the office for ordinary situations, there is not enough equipment or inside and outside lines in any central place to serve for emergency communication.

A crisis checklist

—*Telephone service:* Do you have the capability to handle the extra load of in and out calls without delays. Does your plan include instructions to employees and to switchboard operators to withhold personal and non-essential calls during emergencies? Do you have switchboard operators on standby?

—*Press room:* Is there a central location that can be given over to the press? It should be easily accessible to reporters, preferably near your public relations department. It should have available telephones, sufficient chairs and desks, typewriters, paper and other supplies. You should offer coffee and food if necessary.

—*Radio communications:* Do you have a short-wave, Citizens Band or other radio system that could be used if power or telephone service is lost? Arrangements to monitor the radio should be made with other offices or plants and police and fire departments. Top executives and spokespersons should have portable radios of their own.

—*Electronic bullhorns:* Keep at least one bullhorn or portable public address system in your public relations office or with emergency equipment.

—*Central communications:* Members of your staff should be assigned to central locations and serve as relays for messages.

ASSIGNING TASKS

If possible, your principal spokesperson should stay in one place, near the press room. Other staffers should be responsible for going out into the field; The crisis communication person will have to handle the entire gamut of decisions and questions, and no time should be wasted in finding him.

Someone should be stationed at the building or plant entrance to direct media to the press room and relatives and friends to some other quiet, segregated area. *Keep members of the media, families and victims apart.*

The media spokesperson should be available at the press room, and have authority to answer questions fully and frankly within predetermined limits and be able to make on-the-spot decisions and arrangements necessary for news coverage.

A competent public relations professional should also be stationed in the room to which visitors and relatives have been directed, with instructions to answer questions as positively as possible and with appropriate discretion.

Assign a "floater" to tour all posts and other vital areas to check on how things are being handled. The floater should report to the principal spokesperson regularly with comments and suggestions.

Anticipate the type of questions the spokesperson will probably face. There has to be *some answer* to each of them, even if it is no more than "We don't know yet." A "no comment" is a disastrous response. (See Chapter 12.)

Put the plan in writing! Don't rely on everyone to remember what to do. The plan should be given to each person with a specific assignment, to key officers, to plant and branch office managers, to the head of the safety department, to gate keepers, doormen and security guards. And don't overlook the telephone operators.

Rehearse! Run a disaster drill, and analyze the results. Fine-tune the plan and give special attention to those persons—or areas—where problems arose.

THE PRESS CORPS TOUR

The press corps will probably ask to visit the site of the incident. Plan in advance, taking into serious consideration the following questions:

- Is there any personal danger—hot embers, escaping gas or fumes, the possibility of collapse?

- Might a visitor inadvertently disturb evidence that would hamper official investigations by police, fire, safety and insurance officials?

- Assuming you can take the time, the area is safe and all investigations are completed, is a company official available to escort the press personally?

- If you go on a tour, would any equipment such as flashguns or recorders pose a danger due to combustible fumes?

- Might there be an alternative to a tour? Photographic blow-ups, or floor plan sketches? Can you offer a helicopter ride over the site?

- Can you assemble persons who performed heroic acts so the press can interview them? (Make certain that any person speaking to the press is fully briefed on the latest status to avoid any discrepancies.)

YOUR COMPANY'S IMAGE

Your overall message must be that your company is in control, concerned, and cooperative.

Try to avoid hostile confrontation. If you do become involved in discussions with persons directly involved or with representatives of groups, try to work with them and maintain a cool, professional and concerned position.

Be sure that any technical or operational persons who answer press questions stick to their areas of expertise and don't stray into policy or hypothetical questions.

Guard against questions that try to move from the specific incident at hand to more general areas. You've had a loading dock collapse; this says nothing about your fire-safety or toxic-chemical handling procedures.

Be as absolutely positive as you can of any announcement you make or answer you give. If you do find you have given incorrect information or if a situation changes, inform the media immediately and explain what has happened.

Be certain that the flow of information to top officers of your company is not lagging behind the flow going to the media.

And finally, remember that good will from the press is not a gift. It must be earned. Be honest and accurate and cooperative and the coverage of your company cannot fail to be helped.

THE CRISIS INTERVIEW

The reporter needs you for his or her story. Be honest and responsive while maintaining control.

- As in any interview, know what your principal message is and work it into your answers early and often. (See Chapter 12.)

- Try to respond in headlines and quotable quotes. Get your main facts up front in every answer.

- Don't permit a reporter to shove a microphone an inch or two from your mouth. Simply take your hand and gently move the microphone away, or back away. The reporter will soon get the message.

- Have a way out of an interview should it begin to run too long. Stick to the facts and don't "wing it." If you don't know an answer, say so and offer to get back with details. Don't evade a question and never say "no comment."

- Don't let a reporter reinterpret what you've said in a subsequent question. Correct the question before you attempt an answer. Similarly, don't use a reporter's words unless they are proper.

- If a factual question puts you in a negative light, acknowledge this and then move immediately to a discussion of how you are correcting the situation.

- Be fully prepared for "banana peels" (Chapter 12).

- Don't fall victim to a "speed-up" technique in which a reporter shoves a microphone back and forth rapidly between you. Comment on the microphone's movements lightly, or take hold of the reporter's hand.

- Watch out for a "stall" technique in which the reporter leaves the microphone in your face after you answer, hoping for you to say more. Say what you want to say and no more.

- Don't feel you have to rush into a response; pausing to take a sip or water or some other delaying device can be helpful.

- Don't interrupt a reporter's question unless it is absolutely necessary. You may be stealing your own thinking time. If a reporter interrupts your response, tell him or her politely but firmly that you want to finish.

- Try to spread the interviews around to all of the reporters. Don't play favorites—it could easily backfire.

- At the end of the interview, restate your key points.

AFTER THE CRISIS

Analyze your performance. Examine logs kept during the crisis. Check the information your company gave out and compare it hour by hour to media coverage. How well did the plan work? Could it have worked better?

Inform the press about your efforts to restore operations and to care for the injured.

And distribute "thank you" notes to the media, to the emergency workers and to your own staff; that step should fit it in with your overall effort to show your company's "class."

PART 4

Additional Situations and Skills

CHAPTER **19**

Meetings and Teleconferences

ARE YOU BEING "MEETINGED" TO DEATH?

On the average, executives spend between 50 and 80 percent of their time in meetings. How well that time is spent is another matter. Our experience indicates that, increasingly, executives are taking a close, hard look at the necessity and quality of their meetings.

And they should. While scores of books, manuals, and seminars address this subject, few treat well the nitty-gritty problems that make too many meetings forums for frustration rather than for fruitful discussion and decision making. The advice that follows should be helpful in strengthening standing committees, ad hoc meetings and teleconferences.

First, how carefully have you defined the purpose of your meeting? Is the major purpose to:

—share information
—project a particular image (such as interest, leadership, strength, or decisiveness)
—gather information
—make recommendations

—provide an outlet for cathartic relief
—generate a "political benefit" by granting further access to you, or
—make decisions?

Think about this question carefully, for often when I pose it to executives, they often react with a pregnant pause followed by an admission that they haven't thought enough about their meeting goals. Look at each of the purposes listed above and decide which applies and which doesn't. Then evaluate the intrinsic value of each purpose on a 1–5 scale. (And, of course, there may be other purposes not noted here.)

Next, ask yourself, "How successfully is each purpose being accomplished? Is the meeting the only way—or the best way—to accomplish it?"

Once I help executives relate to this process, they soon learn—often to their dismay—that other regular meeting attendees have different—even conflicting—perceptions regarding the purpose of the meeting. For this reason, I often advise clients to formulate and then circulate a statement articulating its purpose.

THE LINEUP AND THE BATTING ORDER

If you've decided that the regular meeting is destined for survival, then you must ask yourself, "Is it properly composed?" "Do I need my best and my brightest?" "Are there too many or too few committee members?" Again, answering these questions is no easy task, especially in a large organization where being selected or not transmits to the executive all kinds of personal political messages—particularly regarding his or her perceived value to the chairman and, of course, his or her promise for successfully climbing the corporate ladder.

How large the committee should be depends on several factors, including the purpose of the meeting, the extent to which various divisions of the corporation need to be represented, and the hard political reality of preserving egos and preventing their bruising. If the committee's principal purpose is to arrive at major recommendations or to make major decisions not discussed in other settings, nine members is probably the upper limit, with 5–7 being the ideal. However, if the committee is established primarily for reporting and general sharing, it can afford to be larger.

In selecting individuals to serve on standing committees, ask yourself: "Does this person understand what this committee means to me personally?" "Is my accountability in chairing this committee clearly perceived by the committee members?" Indeed, in so many corporations an executive's destiny is significantly tied to his ability to extract from the meetings ideas that can impress his superiors. And, if you have any doubt about how clearly your accountability is being perceived, make it known to the committee as a whole or to the members individually.

THE AGENDA AND THE ENVIRONMENT

Successful meetings normally require careful planning. Crucial to the planning process is the preparation of an agenda. Consider these questions as part of your preparation process:

1. Should an agenda be prepared in advance?
2. If so, should agenda items be invited from the meeting participants?
3. When should the items be invited? By whom? (You, your secretary, the meeting secretary?)
4. How explicitly should the items be stated? Note: I often recommend that the items be phrased as objective questions accompanied by a short statement of justification for inclusion on the agenda.
5. How far in advance of the meeting should the agenda be circulated?

The importance of the meeting environment must not be underestimated. How conducive is it to quality communication? Is the room large enough—but not too large? Is the table shaped to allow the participants to see each other easily? Are chairs comfortable? Should coffee, tea or soft drinks be available? Is the room conducive to standup presentations, including the use of visual aids?

Who sits where in relation to you, the leader, is often a power game. You must decide whether or not you want to control the game. Do you want your closest and most trusted advisers next to you, or doesn't it make any difference? Phrased another way, if you don't take control, do you mind if the person most capable of giving you ulcers is seated next to you?

If you decide to take control, you may be issuing a potentially strong implicit statement about the status of each committee member. Do you want to be—or need you be—concerned with the implications of this control on their egos? Round tables alleviate many problems related to this issue, but the hard reality is that few boardrooms feature round tables.

YOUR LEADERSHIP SYTLE

What kind of tone do you establish when you enter the meeting room? Do you strike the right balance between being sociable and being task-oriented? And do you set the proper example by arriving on time?

Leadership styles have been traditionally placed in three categories: autocratic, democratic, and laissez-faire. Normally, the autocratic leader demands almost absolute control of the discussion, the delegating and the decisions. The democratic leader has a "sharing orientation," regularly soliciting counsel regarding direction and decision-making. The laissez-faire leader (an uncommon commodity in the corporate environment) calls the meeting to order and "goes with the flow"—exercising little if any authority.

Usually a combination autocratic-democratic approach works best. Often, the leader may be more autocratic about the process of moving the meeting along, but democratic in soliciting the views of others, particularly if his respect for them is high.

One of the more frequent stumbling blocks facing leaders of meetings as far as leadership style is concerned is their inability to differentiate between being a traffic cop and a resource person— injecting their points of view into the discussion prematurely rather than first soliciting and listening carefully to the views of others. Moreover, the tendency to inject personal viewpoints prematurely often manifests itself more as pontification or condescension rather than as quality policy input. The net result—a meeting climate crippled by defensiveness—gripped by self-protection to prevent self-destruction.

SYSTEMATIC DISCUSSION AND DECISION-MAKING

When addressing a policy question, e.g., "Should we decentralize our computer operation?", consider the value of conducting a problem-solving analysis:

Problem Analysis A. Is there a problem with our centralized system?
   1. If so, what are its effects?
      a. From a time/cost standpoint?
      b. From a morale standpoint?

Causal Analysis B. What aspects of the centralization are contributing most to the problem? To what degree?

Solution Analysis C. Can adjustments be made to prevent the necessity of decentralizing? How easily? Their potential effectiveness? Cost?

Solution Analysis D. If not, what type of decentralizing design should we consider? To what extent does this resolve the problems addressed earlier? To what extent might it invite additional headaches? Or provide unexpected benefits?

While the example above is but a shorthand version of the many issues that could be raised in contemplating decentralization, the main point is this: *sound decision-making normally dictates that we define a problem and its causes before we even consider a solution.*

In treating each issue and each agenda item you should find the following advice helpful.

1. As you proceed through the decision-making process, check for consensus: "Do we all agree that we have a serious problem with centralization and that problem is . . . ?"
2. Take care to allow each person's idea to be discussed to its logical conclusion. Many meetings are collections of randomized thoughts searching desperately for a unifying comment.
3. From time to time take a few moments to summarize the meeting's progress. It reinforces the quality of the meeting, helps keep everyone on track, and insures a better set of minutes (which, normally, should be taken for standing committee meetings).
4. If you have a tendency to assert your ideas prematurely or your dominance unduly, try converting your assertions into questions. Usually, the results are remarkable—a freer, more positive flow of ideas.
5. If you decide to establish a Task Force composed of selected meeting attendees, consider conducting the selection process in the privacy of your office. Conducting this process during the

meeting itself can only embarrass the rejected members who wanted to be chosen. In addition, prepare a written "mission statement" for the Task Force, indicating deadlines and reporting times. Indeed, too many Task Forces die because of ill definition and poor follow-through by the executive who created them.

Two of the more frequent obstacles to an effective meeting are the monopolizer and the opposite, the reluctant participant. In handling the monopolizer, consider the following options:

1. Interrupt him midflow to indicate politely that everyone understands what he is saying.
2. Interrupt him midflow with a question that can be addressed to someone else.
3. Establish less frequent eye contact with him.
4. Or, as a last resort, speak with him privately, or ask someone else to—someone who may have his ear and who may be less prone to bruise his ego.

For the reluctant participant:

1. Call on him directly to participate, particularly regarding his expertise.
2. Reward quality contributions with genuine positive reinforcement.
3. Go around the table for comments, thereby "forcing" his turn.
4. Speak with him privately—or ask someone else to.

As a final word of advice, too seldom do executives solicit input regarding the quality of their meetings. Indeed, an occasional "meeting about the meeting" may be in order, or individual meetings with participants about the meeting, or a survey, or, of course, all of the above. The amount of time executives spend in meetings requires this all-too-ignored process of self-study—to prevent them from being "meetinged to death."

THE ELECTRONIC MEETING

There was a time when most business was conducted by letter. Meetings were much too expensive because of the time and effort involved in gathering people together.

Then came the rapid growth of our modern economy, and the simultaneous development of the airline industry, and it became possible to hold meetings almost anywhere in the nation and bring people in and out in one day.

But now the costs of doing business have caught up with many companies again. The cost of travel and the value of time spent in getting from place to place—even on a jetliner—have caused a rethinking of priorities.

Technology, in this instance some of the same advances that have come to electronic journalism, has begun to offer a solution for many businesses—teleconferencing.

The sophistication of teleconferencing can vary from an extended conference telephone call to a color and sound private television broadcast. Your company can use the technology for board meetings, staff meetings or addresses to employees. Your public relations department can use a teleconference to hold simultaneous news conferences across the nation.

PREPARING FOR A TELECONFERENCE

What exactly is a teleconference? Present technology now makes it possible to have such things as these:

- Multi-station telephone conference calls using ordinary phones or sophisticated amplifiers and microphones that greatly increase audio quality.
- Slide shows, videotapes and other visual aids, which, shipped in advance to meeting sites, can complement an audio teleconference.
- Transmission of facsimiles of documents via telecopier; hard-copy printouts of images from television screens at each conference site; and direct computer-to-computer electronic mail so that papers can be sent to participants before, during or after a meeting.
- "Electronic blackboards" which can transmit drawings as they are made from one location to another.
- Links to dozens of locations around the country and the world through color television and sound.

The above list is ordered by level of complexity, although technology is advancing so rapidly in this area that the full video conference—already in limited use—should be easily available to any company soon.

You should investigate the services of one of the many consultants already working in this field. Many will assume all the details of setting up a conference, including the temporary or permanent installation of necessary equipment and rental of rooms in remote locations. Several major national motel chains have begun offering video conferences employing the same satellite dish technology used to bring in pay television movies to their guests.

AT&T, which first introduced the concept back in 1964 with its "Picturephone" service (an idea that raced well ahead of the technology at that time), has jumped back into the market with a network of video teleconferencing sites around the nation. The initial trial of the Picturephone Meeting Service Rooms connected New York City, Washington, Philadelphia and San Francisco. The company planned expansion to 58 other points around the nation in 1983 and 1984.

The service is not cheap; in some cases AT&T's offering is more expensive than travel costs (a one-hour session at the company's facility in Philadelphia in 1982 ran up a bill of $2,380). But the more important factor for many businesses is the savings in travel time for executives.

SETTING UP A TELECONFERENCE

Setting the time for a teleconference can involve a massive juggling act. You must find a time convenient to all the participants, bearing in mind that 9 a.m. in New York is 6 a.m. in Los Angeles, 3 p.m. in Paris and 11 p.m. in Tokyo.

You should prepare a clear agenda that includes a specific list of objectives for the meeting and send it to all participants. Any written materials available in advance should be sent on at this time as well. A list of all the participants, their titles and their locations is also of great value.

The chairperson of the teleconference should give some thought to the psychology of the meeting. For example, teleconferences that discuss facts, ideas, or schedules, or engage in problem-solving are generally more successful than those that involve negotiations, bargaining or conflict resolution.

Also, conferences are usually more successful if the participants have previously met face to face.

Of course the missing elements in a teleconference are eye

contact and the visual elements of audience feedback. Some of this can be transmitted via a video conference.

In any case, participants are often unsure of their social or political position in the teleconference, which includes their ability to interrupt and their range of freedom.

The chairperson should remain neutral, acting as a "host" and encouraging each participant to share equally in the meeting. One way to overcome "mike fright" is for the chairperson to encourage a brief period of personal conversation back and forth at the start of the conference. This allows the participants to relax, just as they would at the convening of an ordinary face-to-face session.

During the opening discussions, the teleconference operator can work to solve any technical problems.

This process of "assembly" also gives each participant a chance to associate a voice with a name.

THE TELECONFERENCE IS UNDERWAY

At the assigned starting time, the conference chairperson or secretary should call the roll to assure that all the participants are on the line. After that, the leader should identify himself and introduce each of the participants.

If an electronic blackboard is available at each location, it is often valuable to have each participant "sign in" or check off his or her name on a pre-prepared listing. If the conference is using television facilities, a listing of participants can be broadcast, and the speakers' names and locations can be superimposed on the screen as they speak.

All visual aids should be clearly marked with an identifying number and name. If slides are to be used, the chairperson should announce to all participants, as an example, "The next portion of the meeting will refer to the slide presentations I sent you. Please turn on your projectors and advance to slide number one."

The chairperson should always attempt to address each participant by name; it helps to reduce the artificial barrier and identifies the speaker to the other participants.

The conference should have a specified duration. If the conference must go on for several hours, breaks should be scheduled so that participants can talk informally or leave the room and return when the meeting starts again.

At the conclusion of the meeting, the chairperson should summarize all the main elements in the conference and reiterate any decisions made. After a formal end to the meeting, the lines should be kept open for a while to allow informal discussion—just as people tend to talk to each other about a meeting as they walk out the door.

CHAPTER 20

Executive Testimony

Presenting testimony before a regulatory or legislative body offers a highly structured—and legally pre-defined—forum for a persuasive presentation.

Testimony is the presentation of facts, opinions, or, in some cases, arguments to influence a judicial, administrative or legislative body's decisions.

If you are called to testify in a civil or criminal court, some of the discussion about behavior in the witness chair may be of value to you, but this chapter is not meant to serve as instruction on appearances in a court of law.

Clearly, testimony is a form of communication, and your effectiveness as a witness depends upon many of the same factors discussed in chapters on speech presentation and question-and-answer sessions. There are, however, some aspects of testimony that require special attention:

- Testimony is generally given under oath, and witnesses are subject to the laws of perjury in the jurisdiction involved.

- Testimony is usually presented in a true adversarial setting, in which other participants have a direct, financial interest in the proceedings.

- Presentation of testimony is generally subject to "rules of evidence," a sometimes peculiar body of rules governing style and content.

- A witness is usually subject to a unique—and sometimes diffi-cult—form of structured questioning and testing referred to as cross-examination.

- The success or failure of testimony can often be measured by tangible results, whether or not the position is accepted or rejected. To put it another way, a corporation or government agency may be more forgiving of an ineffective presentation where the con-sequence is a few days of bad press, than of one where the consequence is the loss of tens of millions of dollars.

In quasi-judicial settings such as utility rate-case hearings, testimony is very much dependent upon the cooperation of the witness and his or her attorney; its effectiveness is almost directly proportional to the extent to which the skills of the witness and the lawyer are coordinated.

Think back on the lessons of the chapter on listening: the stress of being "on the stand" is considerable, and in large part your ability to listen effectively will determine the level of success you will have in delivering your message.

A PRIMER FOR WITNESS AND LAWYER

The lawyer's role

The lawyer is ultimately responsible for the outcome of the case. It is his job to determine the legal requirements necessary to bring about a desired result; to communicate those to the witness; to try to make certain that the witness' evidence meets those re-quirements; to assist the witness in direct and cross-examination; to use the witness in cross-examining opposing experts; and to defend or attack a decision in an appeal.

The lawyer and the witness, obviously, must function together as a team:

- The lawyer must alert the witness to the specific require-ments of a regulatory hearing, legislative session or court. There must be adequate time left to prepare and to rehearse.
- You should expect instruction in how to handle peculiar rules of evidence. Is hearsay a problem? If so, it is up to the lawyer to propose a solution. Are the witness' working papers and draft reports "discoverable" by the opposition? If so, you

should be instructed to be careful about committing prelimi-
nary conclusions to paper.

● The lawyer should know the opposition and alert the witness
to any unusual events that may occur. Is the opposing attorney
the type given to histrionics? Will he yell and scream? If so,
practice being calm. Is the opposing attorney not likely to follow
up a question? If so, practice giving short, direct answers.

● Finally, you should expect information on the various rules
of interrogation. For example, what (if anything) can be done
to protect you when you are being cross-examined? Can you
expect your attorney to object when the going gets rough, or
will he stand back so as not to give too much of a tip-off? One
helpful technique is to ask for consultation with your attorney;
if you start this early and often, it may become accepted and
not be regarded as a sign of weakness at difficult moments.

The witness' role

The witness bears the ultimate responsibility of persuading the
decision makers to adopt his or her position.

This is the most difficult task, and it involves more than a
detailed mastery of the subject. It also requires an ability to marshal
all available facts to back up each and every opinion, plus the skill
to present the material in an understandable and convincing
manner.

● You must teach the lawyer the subject matter, and point out
pitfalls and weak spots in his case.
● As a witness, you must help to examine the opponent's case
and assist the lawyer in analyzing it and in cross-examining
opposing experts.
● You must take great care to be consistent with any prior
public statements on the issue. Lawyers will try to turn up past
testimony or publications and use any inconsistencies or contradictions to impeach your credibility. You must let your lawyer
know of any prior work you've done on the subject, and alert
him to any mine fields.
● Finally, you must assist the lawyer in preparing legal briefs.
Has the lawyer included all available facts in support of the
argument? If a critical fact is missing from the record, are there
any accepted reference materials that could be cited?

Presentation of testimony can be looked at as having two
phases—the first "opportunity," and the second "protective." The

ultimate success of a witness' efforts will depend upon the extent to which he or she has taken advantage of the opportunity to present the company's case in the best possible light, and the extent to which he or she avoided the pitfalls thrown in the way by the opposition.

DIRECT TESTIMONY—AN OPPORTUNITY

This is the time to put forth facts or supported opinions without interruption or interference. Depending upon the forum, it may be prepared in advance and presented in writing (administrative and regulatory agencies) or presented orally from the witness stand (courts of law).

Preparation

Know your case. In most cases, you will be just one of several witnesses presented by your side. It is essential that you understand your role as part of the team. Your testimony must be part of an overall theory.

Know your adversary's case. Don't contribute to the opposition when you've got the floor to yourself. If you know what your adversary is trying to prove, you can attempt to avoid giving him a helping hand during your own direct presentation.

Know your forum. Who are the decision makers? What are the rules? Generally, administrative agencies present far more permissive forums than do courts. Rules of evidence and procedure are not applied as strictly. In particular, an administrative or regulatory setting may give you the opportunity to offer "expert" opinions in your testimony for which a court of law might find you unqualified.

Identify your image and substance goals. What is the most important goals you need to accomplish? Tailor your message to address the issue.

Know what you want to say. The most obvious element of preparation is to know thoroughly the facts or opinions you will present in your direct testimony. If you are being questioned by your own attorney and you are aware of an important issue or fact that has not been raised, you have the responsibility to do so. While your answer may appear to be out of place, all that really matters is that the fact or opinion become part of the record of the proceeding; it does not matter how it got there.

Presentation

Be clear. Direct testimony has only one purpose—to communicate facts or opinions favorable to your side. No matter how well prepared a witness is and no matter how thorough the witness is in presentation, the entire process is meaningless unless the decision-maker understands the facts and the message.

Avoid technical jargon as well as oversimplification. You should assume that your audience is mature and intelligent, but knows little or nothing about the subject matter of your testimony.

Be yourself. Don't put on a role which is not natural for you. Your purpose is to present material facts and opinions; it is not to entertain.

Don't vary the script. You and your attorney should have rehearsed your appearance, particularly for oral testimony presented from the witness stand. Don't make changes in the heat of the moment.

CROSS-EXAMINATION:
MAKE IT AN OPPORTUNITY, TOO

Your primary assignment when under cross-examination is to avoid undoing all the positive and productive accomplishments of your direct testimony. Beyond that, you may be presented with or stumble across an opportunity to repeat and reinforce portions of your direct testimony. Be prepared to take advantage of these opportunities.

It is important to understand the purposes of cross-examination: first, to reduce the effect or to impeach the credibility of your direct testimony in the eyes of the decision maker by attacks on you or your testimony; and second, to try to get you to agree with some element of the overall theory of your adversary's case.

Almost every attorney has been taught two basic rules of cross-examination: (1) that a lawyer should never ask a question to which he does not already know the answer, and (2) that all questions should be leading questions—that is, they should suggest a particular answer.

As in direct examination, you should know the overall theory of your side's case so that you can recognize attempts to impeach any aspect of the case. These attempts can be indirect. For example, you might be asked a question that appears to have no bearing on your own testimony, but may in effect impeach the testimony of another witness for your side.

Preparation

Review the past. You must assume that anything you've ever said or committed to print can and will be used against you by an effective cross-examiner. Review previous testimony for contradictions or for changes in fact or policy. Be sure to advise your own attorney of your history.

Anticipate the questioning. Almost every case contains some weaknesses, and your opposition will seek to exploit them during cross-examination. If the weaknesses are obvious, one tactic is to discuss them in the most favorable light in your direct presentation. If the weaknesses are more subtle, you must assume that the opposition will recognize them and attempt to use them. You should anticipate the most damaging possible questions and come up with answers to neutralize them.

Once you've formulated an appropriate answer, make notes of the points you want to use. But don't memorize the exact phrases. At best, a memorized answer may make you appear programmed; at worst, if your memory fails you could look as though you've had a mental short-circuit.

Your attorney should work with you in practice sessions simulating your appearance on the witness stand. One practice that has become increasingly popular is to select a speech communication expert and an additional attorney as consultants. Preferably, the attorney should be someone who has represented opposing interests in the specific administrative jurisdiction involved. You should guard against the appearance of conflict of interest. In addition, you should also seek some kind of protection against the possibility that this attorney will someday turn around and face your company in a subsequent proceeding.

PRACTICE SESSIONS

Your practice session should be as close a duplication of the real setting as possible. Set up the tables and chairs in a conference room to simulate the positions of the hearing officer and opposing counsel. If television crews are possibly expected, use high-intensity lighting in the room. (If your company has video equipment, record the session for review.)

Go through your presentation. Your counsel should offer the same sort of assistance he will be able to give at the actual hearing—no more and no less. Your "outside" legal consultant should play the role of opposing attorney and be as realistic and as demanding as possible.

UNDER CROSS-EXAMINATION

Of course you're nervous. Who wouldn't be? In fact, if you're not nervous, that may be a danger signal. Tension is a sign and a product of the ability to think. The nervousness will not last. As the questions are fired at you in cross-examination, you will quickly begin thinking about the subject rather than about yourself.

Trust yourself. You know who you are and that your abilities have brought you to the position you hold. And you know you have been called to answer questions because you know the answers. Do your job!

Here are some suggestions for your behavior on the stand:

Don't be disarmed: Many witnesses are thrown for a loop when confronted by a cross-examining attorney who adopts the style of a favorite uncle or a naive and stumbling rube. He may well be one or the other, but remember no matter how nice, charming or helpless a cross-examiner may appear, he is paid to tear your case apart—and you with it if necessary.

Don't be intimidated: Remember that you will be facing leading questions and loaded questions. If you believe a simple "yes" or "no" answer is misleading or inadequate, don't hesitate to offer further explanation, no matter how hard the cross-examiner tries to prevent that explanation.

Don't punish yourself: Almost inevitably you're going to make some sort of mistake. Don't dwell on it. Cross-examination can proceed at a very rapid pace, and you will only make the problem worse if you allow guilt or remorse to distract you. Look instead for an opportunity to rehabilitate yourself.

Don't argue: Regardless of the provocation, don't engage in an argument. Keep your cool. Even the most inflammatory question should be addressed with composure: ("Yes, my wife is a bookie. But she reports all of her income faithfully on her Federal tax form.") Let the questioner lose his composure—you'll look the better for it.

Don't emote: This is not your chance to display your contempt for lawyers or the judicial process, nor to show your fine wit or discuss your pet peeves. Answer all questions soberly and with dignity.

Listen very carefully to the opposition's questions: Of all the skills you will bring with you to the witness stand, perhaps the most important is your ability to listen. Trick questions ("Are you still beating your wife?") are rarely put forth deliberately. (Beware of "Banana Peels.") However, lawyers do pose ambiguous questions by accident. If you are asked an unclear question and you answer it, your reply is very likely to be unclear. And be assured that at the end of the case, the lawyer for the opposition will argue for *his* interpretation of what you meant, not yours. If the question is not clear, simply throw it back. Say, "I don't understand your question. Can you put it another way?" or "Do you mean . . ." (and then say what you think he meant).

Listen very carefully to your own attorney: In particular, pay attention if your attorney makes an objection to the question posed to you. Often, your attorney will make such an objection with no real expectation that the judge will agree. Instead, it was meant as a signal to you to be particularly careful in responding.

Think before you answer a question: Despite the impression you may have gained from television portrayals of courtroom procedure, a witness is entitled to take a reasonable time to think through an answer. In fact, pausing before answering *every* question is a very good tactic. You may not need much time to answer the question, "How long have you worked for the company?" But if you consistently pause before answering a question you will buy yourself some free time to think when the going gets rough— without appearing to be stalling or searching for an answer.

Don't guess at an answer: If you don't know, say so. "I don't know," or "I'll have to look it up and answer later," or defer to an upcoming witness. That's a much better position to be in than to guess wrongly and give the impression that you're a dunce—or worse.

Don't volunteer unasked-for information: Remember the setting you're in; don't lapse into ordinary social conversation. The opposing attorney may ask, "When did you last hire an industrial engineer?" Going well overboard, you answer, "That was Joe Doakes. We hired him last November at a starting salary of $12,000 a year, but of course he got a raise along with all the other non-union personnel when the strike was over. We always try to adjust the non-union scale when the union rates change." This unnecessary gabbiness is likely to invite the opposing lawyer to ask about the strike, about management personnel policy—perhaps even to demand a ten-year accounting to show whether and to what extent *every* non-union employee was given a raise after each union contract. Is that what you want?

[By the way, the correct answer to that question was, "Last November."]

Tell the truth: It is both the right thing to do and the safe thing to do. Falsification or distortion can only damage your conscience and your corporation.

LEGALITIES YOU SHOULD KNOW

Laws differ in each state and locality, and in each administrative or legislative setting. However, here are some broadly stated general principles you should know:

The burden of proof: In general, if your company is seeking a particular regulatory position—as an example, a utility seeking a rate change—the burden of proof is with your side. The previously approved position, rate or rule is presumed to be reasonable. Therefore, any party seeking to adjust the existing position cannot simply suggest that a change be made. Instead, there is usually the legal burden of persuading the decision-making body that an adjustment is necessary.

The record: In quasi-judicial hearings the decision-making body is normally supposed to limit its consideration to those elements contained in the record of the proceeding. This means that all factual matters necessary to meet the burden of proof must be included. Your side must make a careful analysis of each logical step in your case to make certain that every point is supported by acceptable evidence. If you forget to get a key fact into the record of a regulatory hearing, it is possible to reopen the proceeding for the limited purpose of hearing the omitted evidence; or an affidavit can be submitted setting forth the missing material.

Rules of evidence: The rules of evidence used in courtrooms are almost impossibly complex. Thankfully, the rules used in administrative settings have been greatly simplified. As a general matter, any evidence can be admitted if it is of the type that "responsible persons are accustomed to rely upon in the conduct of serious affairs." Under this test, hearsay evidence is usually accepted, unless it seems too remote. (Hearsay can be briefly defined as "an out-of-court statement by a person not a witness in the proceeding.")

PREPARING YOUR ARGUMENT

Let's look at two different goals: a situation in which you are advocating a change, and a case where you are opposing a proposal. In the first instance, here are three ways to develop your case:

The problem-solution case: When there is a clear, easily described problem, and when you expect only minimal objection to the proposed change, this strategy is often the best.

1. Show the problem;
2. Describe your plan for change in detail;
3. Show that your plan for change will solve the problems you have explained;
4. Discuss any substantial difficulties you might encounter under the new plan, and show how the benefits outweight any minimal difficulties. Don't create a strawman to knock down; it will only work against you in a closely examined argument.

The comparative advantages case: When you anticipate some objection to the suggested change, this format may be preferable.

1. Present the plan for change.
2. Present the advantages that will come if the plan is adopted; show benefits not only to your company but to the general public, the regulatory agencies, the legislature—the parties involved.
3. Show that the plan will, in fact, produce these advantages.

4. Explain away or minimize any substantial difficulties or disadvantages and show how your plan is, on balance, a good one.

The goals case: Use this format where the most hostile opposition is expected.

1. Develop a number of goals that you, the regulatory body and any other party to the case hold in common;
2. Present your plan;
3. Show that the plan will work toward the desired goals;
4. Account for the disadvantages and show that your plan is better on balance.

At other times, you may be opposing a change that an intervenor, or the regulatory body itself, is seeking to impose upon your company. Major case strategies include the following:

The pure refutation case: Your argument is that the people wanting the change have not proven their case. This form attacks the opposition at every possible point in their case. There is no reason shown for the change, the proposed change is vague and unworkable, and the proposed change will produce serious problems for your company and the public.

The "We're doing it fine now" case: Your goal is to show how well your company is now performing. Things are good and getting better—why change? Show all the disadvantages of the proposed new scheme.

The minor adjustment and repairs case: What problems there are can be dealt with with minor changes. It is best to stay with the known, with minor modifications, than to experiment with radical change. The proposed changes will be expensive, time-consuming and unnecessary. On balance, we are better with a modification of the present system.

The counter plan case: You agree that change is necessary, but not the one now being proposed. Here is a different plan, and here are the advantages of our plan and the disadvantages of theirs.

The pure refutation case should rarely be used by itself. When it is well presented, it may serve to negate the opposition's case, but it gives the judge or other decision maker nothing to believe in, or nothing upon which to base a decision in your favor.

CONGRESSIONAL AND LEGISLATIVE TESTIMONY

A legislative hearing is usually more in the arena of politics than matters of fact, but your needs as a persuasive speaker are no less real.

Find out as much as you can about the norms of the committee or subcommittee. For instance, a written statement is almost always requested for the record, but during your appearance it might be common practice to speak extemporaneously on a subject. What are the time limits? How strictly are they enforced?

Determine who is on the committee, and what their particular interests might be. This "audience analysis" of your questioners can pay off, particularly in a political setting. Attending a hearing conducted by the committee, analyzing a hearing transcript—or both—can be an enormous boon to your performance. What kinds of questions are asked? Who seems particularly interested in which issues or types of issues? What is the committee's tendency to use "banana peels"? Who else has spoken or will speak on the issue? What have they said or will they say? How does your position in the "batting order" influence what you need to say?

If you are going to be making a joint appearance, work out a scheme in advance to separate subject matter and to defer questions—sort of a tag-team match!

Don't be afraid to ask the members of the panel a question, whether in search of clarification or merely to indicate your interest in their perceptions. It can draw the committee or subcommittee into your presentation.

Deliver the prepared or extemporaneously prepared testimony with feeling, applying many of the principles discussed in Chapters 5 through 14. In fact, a friend of mine who served for three terms as a congressman told me that the most painful part of his job on Capitol Hill was to attend hearings; there, he complained, he had to subject himself to seemingly interminable sessions marked by lifeless, boring testimony.

Finally, before you say a word, and as this book has stressed throughout, engage in a simulated hearing. It will sharpen your answers and your confidence.

CHAPTER 21

Debates and Panels

How do you adapt your message and presentation when you're part of a structured group, as in a panel discussion or a debate?

The most important thing for you to do is to *understand the structure*. Discuss with the host or moderator—or with your fellow panel members—the ground rules:

1. Who will speak? In what order?
2. Will there be questions from the audience? Who will field them and help maintain control?
3. Can panel members question each other?
4. If this is to be a debate, what is the structure for opening remarks, responses and conclusions?
5. What are the time limits for each speaker or each segment? Who will oversee the schedule? How will speakers be advised as to time taken or remaining?
6. Who will inform the audience of the agreed-upon ground rules?

Remember that the members of your audience are your listeners—not the other participants. Therefore, keep your arguments and your presentation centered on the audience.

The most important element of your presentation, as in every other situation discussed in this book, is your preparation. You must know your subject and be able to establish your authority and credibility before you can enter into the fine points of debate and panel technique. Your preparation should be little different from that for a formal speech, adapting only for differences because of audience analysis and structural considerations. Your introduction, response and concluding remarks are specialized mini-speeches.

In addition to the points you will make in your own presentation, you must work to win your case by responding to and countering points made by your opponents. You can refute or *dissociate* from points that are not relevant or not true. You can *selectively respond* to some but not all of the issues raised. You can *concede* on some minor points graciously, while concentrating on matters of importance.

Here are some tips on technique:

- Be careful not to appear to be overpowering your opponents by sheer force. You should be good enough to be successful in putting across your message and refuting your opponent's message, but do your work with a scalpel, not with a chainsaw. Be particularly wary of situations that might appear to place uneven "weight" on the panel—two against one or three against two participants. Audiences tend to feel sympathy for the apparently overwhelmed underdog. You might consider dropping a member of your team to make the sides appear even; at the very least you should do your utmost to show the audience your sense of fair play.

- Be aware of your non-verbal communication. Sit erect and carefully—don't swivel in your seat or slouch. Listen carefully to the other panelists. You might want to take notes. Your audience should know that you have taken the situation seriously, and you can demonstrate that you have by quoting directly from points made by your opponent. Use normal, expressive gestures.

- Strive for a neutral moderator and location, particularly in a debate situation. The moderator should be the ally of all participants in maintaining order and keeping to the ground rules. It rarely benefits your side to have the moderator obviously favoring you; your audience will hold it against you and your message. Similarly, in most instances it puts you at a great disadvantage to agree to an appearance before an audience that is biased against you.

- In addition to analyzing the audience, you should analyze your opponents. What are their backgrounds? What are their connections to the audience? How well known are they and their opinions? Are they qualified to speak on the subject? What is their manner of presentation? Are there particular areas of strength and weakness in their presentation skills and their knowledge of the subject?

- Prepare your message as you would for any presentation, defining both image and substance goals. You should come back to your principal points often in your remarks, responses and conclusion. Include your message in the questions you ask other panelists.

- Follow the ground rules. Let the other panelists be the ones who exceed time limits or speak out of turn. However, if another participant persists in disregarding the rules and makes a statement you feel must be responded to, insist politely on a fair opportunity.

- Practice for your appearance, simulating the situation as best you can. Videotape your presentations if possible, and make necessary changes.

HAIL TO THE VICTOR (OR WHAT YOU CAN LEARN FROM POLITICAL DEBATES)

Debate is high theater, particularly when the participants are operating under the intense pressure of a political campaign. There is tremendous risk because of the unpredictability of the situation; the potential for great gain exists for the same reason.

I have been involved as an advisor on debating tactics for numerous candidates for high office, including Ronald Reagan in 1980. Though you may or may not see your own campaigns as having the import of a run for the presidency, some of the lessons from the debates are universal.

In your efforts to fulfill your image and substance goals, there are three ways in which you relate to the audience: *physical* (actual movements), *forensic* (argumentative behaviors or ploys), and *tonal* (attitude or tone projected through physical and vocal cues).*

Physical tactics

Getting on stage: Should you take the stage first or wait to make a grand entrance? The first candidate can project his confidence and his eagerness to do battle. However, he could be left anxiously waiting for his opponent. The latecomer can create an air of expectation, which, upon his arrival, allows him to take command of the stage. This was the decision made by Ronald Reagan in 1980. He heightened his command by walking across the

---

*For a more detailed discussion regarding debate strategy and tactics see *Political Campaign Debates: Images, Strategies and Tactics* by Myles Martel, New York: Longman, 1983, pp. 57-115.

stage to shake President Carter's hand. This not only projected an image of command and friendliness for Reagan, but it caught Carter by surprise, and diminished him before 120 million television viewers.

Eye contact: If you are on television, the camera affords the audience a much closer view of your gaze than is received by persons in the room with you. Think about what your eye contact might communicate: sometimes you might not want to watch your opponent when he is speaking for fear that you will communicate too much interest in what he is saying. There are times, too, when a candidate will choose to ignore visually and orally a minor party candidate so as not to give him unwarranted legitimacy. There is a fine line, though, between these tactical considerations and the appearance of disrespect.

During preparations for the 1980 presidential debates, Reagan was advised to look at Carter when expressing righteous indignation. ("There you go again," was Reagan's famous phrase.) He was also advised against looking downward, a tendency he had shown in an earlier debate with John Anderson—a look which suggested a lack of confidence, indecisiveness or lack of preparation.

Notetaking can complement your eye contact tactics. In 1976, President Ford was advised to take notes in his debates with Governor Carter, not only to help him remember points he wanted to make, but also to distract his audience when Carter was saying something with which he disagreed.

A debater may feel it desirable to stare down an opponent or even point a finger at him to communicate willingness to confront him. This tactic is often effective, but can backfire if it is too obvious or showy. In John Anderson's 1980 Illinois Republican primary debate against George Bush, Anderson called his opponent on his behavior: "George, you don't have to point your finger at me. Really, don't get so excited."

Seated or standing?: During the negotiations that led to the 1976 debates between President Ford and Governor Carter, much controversy involved whether the candidates should stand or sit. Carter's aides wanted their candidate to sit on stage, to communicate his informal style. Ford's advisors wanted him to stand, a more "presidential" demeanor. The compromise allowed for stools behind the lecterns.

The proper smile: There is little doubt that the public is impressed with the "nice guy." Looking too serious can communicate a lack of confidence and a feeling of tension. In 1980, Reagan's engaging smile contrasted strongly with Anderson's taut, professorial face and with Carter's edgy, self-conscious appearance. Again, there is a fine line between a friendly smile and a disrespectful smirk.

Forensic tactics

Forewarning: If you can anticipate your opponent's attacks, you might find it useful to forewarn the audience of them and answer them in advance, the "preemptive strike" I spoke of in Chapter 7. "My opponent has been claiming in the campaign that I. . . ."

The shotgun blast or the laundry list: A forceful combination of accusations or questions. This can leave the opponent with too many points to answer effectively, or force him to go on the offensive ill-prepared. The risks are that the opponent will be able to answer the points or be capable of mounting a strong offense of his own, now that you have opened the door to a change in tone.

Turning the tables: Redirecting an opponent's attack back at him can often be successful. "If you are going to try to blame me for everything that went wrong during the past four years, you have got to allow me credit for the things that went right. Let me tell you about some of those. . . ."

Flat denial: Assuming you are dead certain of your facts, a flat denial is a very strong argumentative statement. You can say, "That is not true," or you can combine a denial with an unspoken message, as in Reagan's "There you go again" to Carter.

Tossing a bouquet: In certain instances, it might be advisable to compliment your opponent on conduct in office or during the campaign. This projects an image of fair-mindedness, diminishes impressions that you are overly contentious and makes it more difficult for your opponent to direct a strong attack against you.

Timing: Speaking too long might give the impression of windiness; speaking for too short a time might imply lack of knowledge. Turned around, though, a lengthy answer in certain circumstances is an effective way to answer a question of some controversy—it shows you as a thoughtful, deliberate person. Similarly, a short, concise answer can contrast sharply with an overly wordy and confusing reply by your opponent.

Tonal tactics

Controlling backlash: Probably the most serious risk faced by a debater, backlash can solidify the opposition and lose uncommitted or weak supporters. Most theorists agree that it is generally inadvisable to attack first, but again it depends upon your relative position in a debate—is your credibility high enough to support your contentiousness?

Avoiding defensiveness: Righteous indignation is the happy medium between too much anger and too much defensiveness. By projecting this trait or tone the debater appeals to the audience's sense of fair play as he diminishes the potential for backlash.

What do you call your opponent? There are five common forms of address, each with different implied messages:

"My opponent." This establishes a cold distance between you and your opponent. This tactic might not be advisable if the situation has not been polarized and particularly if your opponent is so popular or holds such a powerful position that referring to him coldly would imply disrespect.

"Mr. (Miss, Mrs. or Ms.) Jones." This communicates respect and distance.

"The governor ..." (commissioner, director, etc.) This may tend to subordinate you to your opponent's position and in many cases is inadvisable. However, it can be effective if your goal is to remind the audience of just that—that your opponent is responsible for what you are attacking. Be especially careful to make it clear that it is the office holder and not the office that is being criticized.

"Governor (Commissioner, Director) Jones." This form also emphasizes your opponent's position, but in a less cold and formal manner. It has the same advantages and disadvantages as the previous example.

"Jimmy." First names are generally used to diminish the stature of an opponent, and less often to suggest informality and warmth. Ronald Reagan referred to Congressman Anderson as John during their debate, a tactical decision. Of course, you and your opponent may use first names if you know each other personally—and if the audience is aware of this. However, be wary of using first names in any other circumstance.

How do you refer to yourself? "I" communicates acceptance of responsibility and the strength of your role in your company or administration, but it can also convey conceit and selfishness. "We" is the word of the team player, implying openness to advice and the ability to work in cooperation with others, but "we" can also imply weakness and an unwillingness to accept responsibility.

CHAPTER 22

Special Situations and Issues

IN EXTRAORDINARY SESSION

"We're gathered here for a special occasion, to:

	introduce
	honor
	praise
Choose	nominate
one:	accept
	bury
	eulogize
	commemorate
	or be entertaining.

If one of these is your assignment, then before you say a word you should give some thought to the special demands and opportunities you will face.

Included in this group are five basic types of speeches: praise, introduction, entertainment, presentation and acceptance.

If there is one rule that can be applied to special occasion speeches, it is that there are no rules. But there are principles you can apply to improve the reception of your remarks.

SPEECHES OF PRAISE

These include commemorations of great events or individual accomplishments, dedication of buildings or places (Lincoln's Gettysburg Address came at the dedication of the cemetery at that Civil War battlefield), eulogies and nominating speeches.

- You have no right to make a speech of praise if you don't know your subject. You can offer no credibility, and you serve only to demean the object of your praise if you cannot establish your personal knowledge or research.

- Your remarks must be appropriate to the occasion and the subject. This does not mean there is a set pattern established somewhere for every situation (not all funeral eulogies are funereal; the burial of some of the comedians of our age have been accompanied by appropriate one-liners; the burial of great musicians has been done to the sound of swing). Just be sure that you take the time to consider your message before you say a word.

SPEECHES OF INTRODUCTION

Such speeches can range from a short presentation of a principal speaker or the members of a panel to a speech that serves to set the agenda and tone for an entire conference.

- Here, too, you should know the person you are introducing. Nothing is more deadly boring than listening to someone stumbling his way through a recitation of a resumé. Your role as introducer is a serious one; you are there to help the speaker by answering some of the audience's questions: Who is this person who wants to talk to us? Obtain a copy of his resumé or biography. What are his or her credentials? What is the subject? You should take the time to do some research and to prepare a mini-speech of persuasion to help the speaker who follows you with his own task.

- Don't steal the speaker's thunder with your introduction. You're there to fit in with the speaker's plan, not to sabotage it. Say just enough to help establish the speaker's credibility and to whet the audience's appetite. You might want to consult with the speaker (you have been introduced, haven't you?) before you both go on stage to be certain your planned remarks are appropriate. If you're the speaker, you should seek out your introducer to find out what he or she will say. The point is that you are not there to air your own views on the subject. You are the speaker's advance man—your job is to warm up the crowd and then step aside.

- In preparing the introduction, think about personal qualities the speaker exemplifies and consider building your remarks around them. Some of the more popular touchstones: civic responsibility, commitment to party, courage, management know-how, dedication, problem-solving ability, financial acumen, scholarship, generosity, etc.

- Be reasonably brief, but include your name, the speaker's name and a bit about the topic. If there are any special ground rules or format, like a question-and-answer session to follow the address, you can announce that.

- Many successful speeches of introduction play off the old clichés: "Without further adieu..." or, "It gives me great pleasure to introduce..." or "Let's greet...." Stale though they are, such lines seem to add a touch of show biz and help gain attention to you and your speaker.

- And here's a note you might want to bear in mind for your own speaking appearances: you can take control of the situation by offering to the host a "suggested" speech of introduction you've written yourself. Send it on ahead of the speech, and bring a second copy with you in case your introducer has mislaid it. What better way of enhancing your own credibility before you speak than by writing the introduction yourself or having your speech-writer do it for you.

SPEECHES OF ENTERTAINMENT

These speeches are obviously in a class of their own, and generally require highly developed skills. As mentioned earlier, though, a distinction must be drawn between using jokes and using humor. It takes a comedian to do the former well; a well-prepared speaker can do the latter. Whatever material you gather or invent on the spot, if you are not at least 85–90% confident that the humor is appropriate or funny, forget it. There are no statues or plaques commemorating the "comedians" who bombed in Boston—or anywhere else. But our memories can store too well a tasteless remark intended to be humorous. (See discussion of humor in Chapter 9.)

SPEECHES OF PRESENTATION AND SPEECHES OF ACCEPTANCE

These should be well known to us all through their regular appearance on one or another of the endless stream of awards shows on television. It should also be apparent to us all that some of them are done well and some of them speak poorly of the presenter and the presentee.

- The best responses are almost always those which, though short, nevertheless represent the fruits of careful thought and planning. Once again, thinking about themes or traits (as with a speech of introduction) should suggest clear, genuine, comfortable—and touching—phrases.

- Remember your message. If it's to say "Thank you," say so graciously and briefly. If others are to be thanked, do so modestly—and briefly.

HOW LONG IS LONG ENOUGH?

Again, there are no hard and fast rules. Are you the principal speaker, the main attraction? Or are you part of a whole evening's program? What time of day? Has the audience just eaten? Is the audience waiting for dinner?

The *principal speaker* could legitimately lay claim to 20–30 minutes. So, too, a speaker before a college class or a seminar.

An *after-dinner* speech should be light in weight and short in length, otherwise it falls on sleepy ears. While an ordinary presentation might be 20 minutes or more, you might find 15 minutes to be the top limit for a post-prandial presentation.

An *after-lunch* speaker should be aware of the plans of the audience. Are they expecting to get back to their businesses for an afternoon of work? Are there other events to come that day? Are the participants hoping to leave before the evening rush hour?

It is, by the way, better to be too short than too long. You'll earn the gratitude of your host and your audience if you take slightly less than your allotted time, since most meetings seem to run behind schedule.

ARRANGING FOR A GUEST SPEAKER

Here's your chance to observe the biblical injunction: Do unto other guest speakers as you would have done unto you.

- Before the appearance, confirm all arrangements in writing if possible, including the date, time, location and topic. Make clear the nature of the program: what does the audience expect to hear? A humorous presentation? A commemoration? A serious paean? Inform the speaker about the formality of the session: are wives or husbands invited? Will the press be invited? Will there be a question-and-answer session?

- While you're on the subject, ask the speaker to provide biographical information, photographs, advance texts and other information where appropriate.

- Basically, you should outline for the speaker all of the answers to the questions you should ask before you go on stage for a presentation of your own. (See Chapter 6.)

- It would also be considerate to bring up the subject of honoraria and expenses, hotel arrangements and transportation provisions.

- And finally, you should offer to perform whatever services are necessary to assist your speaker in making a persuasive presentation. Arrange to rescue him from a hostile audience if necessary; if he wants, arrange for a cut-off at a specified time.

GOING TO THE EXPERTS

You're standing at the front of a room, squinting into the glare of television lamps. A bouquet of microphones is arranged on the podium. Before you—some standing, some seated, some politely extending an index finger, others violently waving arms or notebooks—are a dozen reporters.

They all begin yelling at the same moment:

"What are you going to do about...?"
"When did you first learn...?"
"Will you call for an evacuation...?"
"Why did your company allow this to happen...?"
"How could this sort of gross negligence occur...?"

You choose one of the questions to answer, but you are interrupted—first by a technician who walks in front of you and holds a light meter in your face; next by a late-arriving radio reporter who tries to tape his microphone to your notebook; and finally by an impatient television "star" at the back who insists that you answer his question now.

Is this every spokesperson's worst dream? Quite possibly. But in this instance, you're paying for the privilege of the abuse.

The "reporters" in this scene are trained consultants; the "television crews" are filming you to allow you to see your reactions to stress and to help you learn; the "disaster" script you're working from is one that comes from the real possibilities inherent in your own company.

The scene comes from a training session of one of the professional communication consultants available to executives.

Besides the press conference simulation (and it feels like no simulation at all to the participant), there are demonstrations of talk shows, one-on-one interviews with a reporter, telephone interviews and crisis training. The speech presentation portion of the course includes impromptu delivery, speeches from notes, speeches from outline and other situations. All work is videotaped and critiqued, and participating companies can obtain copies of the tapes for further use after the seminar.

Courses also include handling yourself on stage, non-verbal communication, clothing and grooming tips, and use of visual aids.

Do you need to engage the services of a professional consultant? You regarded the subject of executive communication to be important enough for you to read this book. Consider a consultant as a postgraduate course.

Here are some criteria to consider when you consider engaging a consultant:

- Will he be accessible to you when you need him?
- Is he a person you feel you can share personal and corporate intimacies with?
- Does he have an academic or professional background in the electronic media, speech theory and journalism?
- Is he as well attuned to substance—to your issues—as to form?
- Who are his clients and what do they think of him?
- What has he written and are you impressed with what he has to say?
- Has he faced large audiences, been interviewed on talk shows?

- Do the formats for his programs make sense?
- Does he specify learning objectives to be accomplished through his programs?
- And, of course, are his fees reasonable?

SHOULD YOU HIRE A SPEECHWRITER?

You've got counsel to handle your legal affairs. You've got an accountant to take care of the books. You've got an appointments secretary to keep track of your schedule. If you speak frequently, you may need to hire a speechwriter.

You *can* benefit from the assistance of a professional writer if you are willing to work *with* him or her during preparation, and then take over the speech and make it yours before delivery.

How do you choose a speechwriter? You are, in effect, selecting a partner and confidant, a person who will be privy to some of your secrets. You want someone who will not be afraid to tell you when you are not at your best, or afraid to make suggestions.

You also want someone who knows the business: how to conduct research, the meaning of a "deadline," and the way business operates. Not just any "writer" will do, either: he or she must have an ear for oral speech, and perhaps most important, the ability to adapt his or her writing to your tone and style.

YOUR RESPONSIBILITY TO YOUR SPEECHWRITER

Your involvement with a speech must begin well before word one is committed to paper. *You* must be the one who decides what is to be said—not the speechwriter. You should plan on sitting down with the writer—just the two of you—and talking about the subject. Let the writer hear your words and phrases. Provide the writer with basic directions, with a sense of your feelings and thoughts, and with the power to seek out assistance in your name. You must grant the speechwriter ready access to you and to those around you.

You also owe it to your speechwriter to listen to his ideas and suggestions. If he is any good, he will be working hard toward the same goals as you. And then you must take over the final stages—the fine-tuning to meet your style, the outlining and the rehearsals.

After the speech, report back to the writer. Tell him what worked and what didn't work. (An audiotape or videotape of your speech could pay enormous dividends here.) Explain the changes you made so the writing can be fine-tuned for you.

THE ETHICS OF EXECUTIVE COMMUNICATION

The English poet and critic, Alexander Pope, once said, "He who tells a lie is not sensible how great a task he undertakes; for he must be forced to invent twenty more to maintain that one."

Wise and timeless advice for sure. Yet pressures facing today's executives often blur or blind them to the distinction between truth and falsehood. When push comes to shove, can a white lie told by an executive to an audience, to a reporter or to a governmental panel preserve his career path and the corporation's image? Possibly, but the risks are, as Pope alluded, too great—not only the risk of discovery, but also the risk of losing one's own sense of conscience or decency.

The executive must, in reviewing and appraising his ethical standards as a communicator, differentiate between truthfulness and openness. Truthfulness, in essence, means that whatever the executive says is, to the best of his knowledge, factual and free from distortion. Openness implies the extent to which the faucet of factual and interpretative information is opened. Hence, as a communicator, the executive must be absolutely truthful, while his openness should be relative.

In establishing a personal set of standards for ethical communication, the executive should consider the following advice:

1. Double or triple check the sources and, if necessary, the methodology behind ideas or data which register any doubt in his mind.
2. Monitor the tendency to distort a reality through the selective use of numbers or statistics.
3. Scrutinize his logic for any tendency to use fallacies (see Chapter 8).
4. Achieve a sense of security in being able to say "I don't know."
5. Maintain a sense of self-worth by avoiding the temptation to fabricate examples or other data when his case seems deficient.

When setting his standards for ethical communication, the executive should derive additional strength from the well-chosen words of William Penn: "Truth often suffers more by the heat of its defenders, than from the arguments of its opposers."

CHAPTER 23

A Case Study: Johnson & Johnson's Bad Dream

Nightmares can come true, but few companies in recent years have had to deal with a more horrifying experience than did Johnson & Johnson, makers of Tylenol capsules. In 1982, seven persons in the Chicago area died suddenly, with medical links to cyanide ingested in Tylenol capsules.

What would you have done when reporters first began calling? Denied any involvement? Said "no comment?" Continued sales while waiting for final word?

This was no small decision for the huge company. During this crisis Tylenol accounted for about 35 percent of the over-the-counter pain reliever market. If Tylenol were a separate company, its profits before the incident would have placed it in the top half of the Fortune 500 list of major companies.

Johnson & Johnson took the long-range view of the situation. It recognized that it had to hold the trust of the American consumer. Its first step was to remove all its capsule products from the marketplace, first in the Chicago area and then nationwide. It spent more than $100 million on a campaign to issue warnings about the poisonings, and to recall, test and destroy Tylenol capsules.

Almost immediately, the company launched a campaign to regain its good name.

Here are some excerpts from a speech by James E. Burke,

chairman of the company, delivered on Nov. 11, 1982. It is a fine example of a carefully prepared, honest presentation on a highly sensitive subject. It combines reinforcement of the corporate credibility of Johnson & Johnson with a muted expression of outrage.

The remarks were delivered via a live 30-city video conference, with reporters watching across the nation.*

Let me thank you all for joining us today in 30 cities across the country to talk about Tylenol.

In every sense of the term this has become a national tragedy, and everyone in America shares a part of the burden that it imposes.

It will be a long time before the full impact of this senseless crime can be properly assessed, but the changes it has already brought about in our lives are profound.

It has introduced us to a new form of terrorism and brought the potential for new fears and concerns closer to our homes. It has alerted the consumer to new dangers and touched off a revolution in consumer packaging that eventually will reach all areas of the marketplace.

But whatever the impact has been on our individual lives, including the financial strain it has imposed on our company, and the countless ways it has touched the lives of others, let us never forget that the seven victims paid the ultimate price. Nor should we forget the intense sorrow and heavy burden placed upon their families.

You, the news media, were the first to make the evaluation that our company and our product were *also* victims of this tragedy. You have treated us accordingly and we are deeply appreciative.

And now I would like to share with you our perspective on three important elements of the story you are covering:

The past events;
The current situation;
Our plans for the future of this important brand.

I will begin by stating that as a company we have made the *unequivocal commitment* to rebuild this business under the Tylenol name.

It will take time.
It will take money.

*Copyright © 1982. Reprinted by permission of Johnson & Johnson.

And it will be very difficult.

But we are confident that it can and should be done.

Now, let me review the past events—since the tragedy began in Chicago.

The tampering and the poisoning of the product *did not take place in our plant.* The Food & Drug Administration confirmed that after a careful inspection of our manufacturing facilities. The tampering most likely took place in Chicago.

Initially, however, we had no way of knowing that the criminal tampering was confined to the Chicago area. So when the first lot number was identified we notified the Food & Drug Administration and informed the media of the withdrawal of the product from the 34 states where it had been distributed.

We did the same when a second lot was identified in Chicago. We set up emergency phones to answer questions from consumers and health care professionals.

We halted production of capsules, suspended advertising and concentrated on keeping the public informed through the press and government agencies. We then decided that in order to provide maximum protection for the public, all Tylenol capsules had to be withdrawn nationwide. We did that knowing full well the impact of that decision on our business.

We publicized the national withdrawal broadly and told consumers not to take capsules in their possession. We quickly sent more than two million messages to inform health care professionals of the facts and to alert retailers and wholesalers to take capsules off their shelves.

And, to add whatever help it might provide to the authorities investigating the poisonings, we offered a reward for information leading to the arrest and conviction of the person or persons responsible for tampering with the capsules.

At the same time, we set up special laboratories to test Tylenol capsules to detect other cyanide poisonings. As of today, more than a million capsules have been tested by us, the FDA and other agencies. Fewer than 75 capsules—all in the Chicago area—have been found to contain cyanide. But two contaminated bottles were found in Chicago as a result of the withdrawal, so we believe we may have helped to save some lives.

•　•　•　•　•

From the very first call we received from the news media, and throughout the more than 2,000 we have responded to in the ensuing weeks, there was never any question that we would answer your questions honestly, factually and as completely as we could.

We were very much aware that the public welfare was at stake, and that the news media were the means by which we could rapidly disseminate warnings, allay mounting fears and put the crisis in perspective. You will recall that there were many unconfirmed reports of illness, and many false rumors during the early stages. Good reporting helped to reduce these tensions.

The public has been well-served by our joint and cooperative efforts—and again I want to thank you for the part you played.

For our part, we estimate the cost of the early warning we initiated, picking up the products, of testing and destroying the capsules to be approximately $100 million.

But all of that is behind us. What of the present situation?

It is important to understand that loyal customers have continued to use and purchase Tylenol tablets, which were not involved in any tampering.

This in spite of the intensity of the coverage, which has been staggering. According to our surveys, this is what the public was thinking as of this week:

> Knowledge of Tylenol tragedy—94 percent
> Problem involves Tylenol capsules only—90 percent
> Problem could occur for any capsule—93 percent
> Maker not to blame—90 percent.

While there is considerable understanding of what happened, there is also a great residue of fear and anxiety in the hearts of the American public.

A survey of the people who are not regular Tylenol users tells us that close to 80 percent show little interest in ever using the brand. Unless we can change that attitude, we have been deprived of the right to compete for that business.

But among regular Tylenol users, there is extremely positive news, and it continues to get better with each survey report.

●   ●   ●   ●   ●

Now what about our future plans?

First and foremost, our McNeil sales people met with us this week and are now calling on the trade—reintroducing Tylenol capsules in a tamper-resistant package. It will start appearing on store shelves in a few weeks and be in most stores by January 1. This package has three separate barriers to entry and, with the cooperation of alert consumers, affords the public the best protection we could reasonably devise.

This new package for Tylenol capsules is clearly marked: "New Safety Sealed." There is a warning printed on the box: "Do not use if safety seals are broken." The outer box has glued flaps that must be forcibly removed to reach the bottle. That's the first check point.

The bottle . . . has a tight plastic neck seal which covers the cap and neck of the bottle. This neck seal must be torn to remove the cap. That's the second check point.

Finally, there is a strong inner foil seal over the mouth of the bottle, which must be broken to reach the capsules inside. That's the third check point.

Of course, the cooperation of the consumer is important, and again this is another role the media can play.

As Commissioner Arthur Hayes of the Food & Drug Administration has said. . . . there is no such thing as a *tamper-proof* package.

[Videotape of Commissioner Hayes shown.]

•   •   •   •   •

Our second important announcement today is that we plan to replace, free of charge, the Tylenol that our users have thrown away.

Consumers can take advantage of the free offer by calling a special telephone number.

[Display offer on screen.]

We will also be running in newspapers later this month and in December a special free coupon good for $2.50 toward the purchase of any Tylenol product.

In summary, we have tried to relieve anxiety and begin the building process in four ways:

1. We recalled all capsules and they are being destroyed.
2. We communicated with our customers . . . asking for their trust.
3. We are reintroducing our Tylenol capsules in a triple-seal tamper indicator packaging.
4. We are offering to replace any Tylenol user's product through a coupon worth $2.50.

We are developing other plans, of course. But this is our commitment to the loyal consumers of Tylenol who have given us their trust. This loyalty is the biggest reason we have complete confidence in our ability to rebuild this business.

· · · · ·

While we consider this crime an assault on society, we are nevertheless ready to fulfill our responsibility, which includes paying the price of this heinous crime. But I urge you not to make Tylenol the scapegoat.

We consider it a moral imperative, as well as good business, to restore Tylenol to its preeminent position in the market place.

But it is ironic that the job of rebuilding Tylenol is made more difficult because we all—Johnson & Johnson, the regulatory agencies and you, the media—did our job of informing and protecting the nation so efficiently.

· · · · ·

I am confident that the news media, working in its own way and according to its own dictates, will help us to dispel these fears about a product that rightfully earned the confidence of the public. We welcome any help we can get from you and others in the vast rebuilding task that lies ahead.

In the final analysis, we believe that the American consumer, properly informed by the news media, will make an eminently fair decision about the future of Tylenol.

WHY THIS EXAMPLE?

The tragedy of the Tylenol poisonings is a case study of what this book is all about—the difficult, peril-fraught situation handled with great sensitivity, professionalism and decisiveness.

Johnson & Johnson truly waited before it said a word about the Tylenol comeback—not delaying responses that might have endangered any lives nor taking so long as to look indecisive—but taking long enough to make sure that its words were proper and effective. In the face of the most surprising and damaging assault on a major American corporation in recent history, Johnson & Johnson was able to maintain, indeed enhance, its credibility—its reputation for fair and proper dealing—and to control the damage to its position in the marketplace.

These are the lessons we would hope you, the reader, will take from this book.

INDEX

A

Alabama Journal, 130
Alabama Power Company, 130–31
Alliteration, in a speech, 46
Ambiguity, in a speech, 42
Anderson, John, 192, 193
Antimetabole, in a speech, 45
Antithesis, in a speech, 45
Anxiety. *See* Nervousness
AT&T, 174
Attention:
  audience span of, 63, 75
  factors for getting, 63
  faking, 23
  radio and, 146
Assonance, in a speech, 46
Audience:
  attention span of, 63, 75
  hostile, 62, 80
Audience, analysis of:
  age, 58–59
  determine needs of, 60–61
  economic status, 59
  makeup of audience, 55–56
  nationality, 59
  physical arrangements, 57
  religion, 59
  sex, 58
Audio tapes, 113
Avis, 151
Ayer Directory of Publications, 149

B

Bacon's Publicity Checker, 149
"Banana Peels," 100–103, 148
Barron's, 67

B (continued)

Body language, 22, 28–29
  See also Communication, non-verbal
Body motion, 26, 138–39, 144
Borman, Frank, 151
Bradley, Stephen E., 131
Broadcasting/Cablecasting Yearbook, 149
Brothers, Joyce, 149
Burke, James E., 157, 204–9
Bush, George, 192
Business Week, 133

C

Cable television, 146
Cable TV Publicity Outlets Nationwide, 149
Carnegie, Dale, 144
Carter, Jimmy, 103, 192, 193
CEO, 150–51, 160
Chalkboards, 112
Charts, types of, 113
Chronemics, 27
Chrysler Corporation, 150–51
Churchill, Winston, 46, 108
Clarity, in a speech, 42
Close, Jeff, 150
Clothes. *See* Dressing
Colloquialisms, in a speech, 41
Communication, non-verbal, 25–32
  eyes, 27–28
  face, 28
  hands, 28–29
  types of, 26–27
  use of pauses, 31–32
  voice, 29–31
  See also Body language
Complex words, in a speech, 43
CompuServe, 67